The Birds That Saved Me

J. P. Steed

with artwork by
Norah Steed

GHOW Press LLC
Austin, Texas

ISBN: 978-1-960554-00-0

More praise for *The Birds That Saved Me*:

"At times poignant, at times playful, always perceptive, Steed weaves the wisdom of various theologies with poetry, baseball, and ornithological detail in an easy, conversational style. Highly recommended—and don't overlook the footnotes in the back!"

– Ron McFarland, author of *The Rockies in First Person*
and *Appropriating Hemingway*

"A book of beautiful complexity, interweaving personal responses to the world of birds with an astonishing depth of research."

– Mary Clearman Blew, author of *Think of Horses*
and *All But the Waltz*

"5 out of 5 stars. This book is a must-read."

– *Online Book Club*

Praise for Norah Steed:

"[T]his memoir comes to life with the outstanding illustrations by Norah Steed, whose brilliant artwork perfectly complements the author's words."

– *The Midwest Review*

"Norah Steed's colorful, pen-and-ink drawings are fascinating, beautifully bringing the birds alive while adding to the book's appeal."

– *The Prairies Book Review*

"Beautifully illustrated throughout with Norah Steed's brilliant arwork..."

– *BookView Review*

This was for me.
But I hope it helps you, too.

Contents

I know all the birds of the mountains.

– Psalms 50:11

Do you not see the birds above,
spreading their wings and folding them in?
Nothing holds them up but Allah.

– Surah 24:41

And there is no animal on the earth,
nor bird that flies on two wings,
but they are communities like yourselves.

– Surah 6:38

Ask the animals, and they will teach you,
or the birds of the air, and they will tell you.

– Job 12:7

For a bird of the air shall carry the voice,
and that which hath wings shall tell the matter.

– Ecclesiastes 10:20

The End

Sometimes the pain is too much
to examine, or even tolerate.

– Jim Morrison

If I say it was a hard year, you might guess which year I'm talking about. On a depressing day in April 2020—not long after the world shut down—I was moping around the house, listening to "The End" by The Doors. And after I had listened to that eleven-minute-and-forty-one-second song four times in a row, I decided I should go for a walk. So I did. And it helped. So the next morning I got up and went for another walk. And it helped. And just like that, I had a new morning ritual: get up early, go for a walk through the neighborhood, suck the morning air into my lungs, feel the firm concrete beneath my feet, watch the trees flutter. Because it *helped*.

Our family had been through some hard things over the years. My wife and I have raised—and are still raising—five kids. We've seen stitches, broken bones, concussions, surgeries. We've had job struggles, job changes, job losses. We've seen and suffered the effects of abuse and addiction. Disease and trauma. Depression. Death. And the years leading up to April 2020 had been especially hard—culminating in the collective hardship of a worldwide pandemic.

But I'm not going to dwell on the details of our difficulties, because this book is not about the hard things. This book is about the *good* things. The healing things that have helped me to survive the hard things. This book is about finding a new beginning when you feel like you're at The End. This book is about morning walks. About trees, rivers, poetry. And birds.

In April 2020, I started going for walks because I was struggling with hard things. And then I started seeing the birds.

And the birds are what saved me.

Fall

The Spark Bird
Avis scintilla

> When I discover who I am,
> I'll be free.
>
> – Ralph Ellison

Walks are great. I recommend them. Seriously: you should put this book down and go for a walk right now. The book will still be here when you get back. You think I'm joking, but I'm not. Trust me. *Just go.*

Even better than a regular walk is a walk by the water. A river, a stream, a lake, a pond—an ocean—any kind of water. On one of my first walks, I cut across a field behind the elementary school and discovered a path down to a small creek that runs through our neighborhood. (Pro tip: the best walks are not constrained by where the sidewalk ends.) That morning, when I found my way down to the neighborhood creek— where I could crouch on its bank and wet my fingers—I wept. I took off my shoes and socks, rolled up my pants, and waded over to another section of the bank, where I saw another creek spilling through the trees into the creek that I was wading in. And I thought of that Raymond Carver poem:

> The places where water comes together
> with other water. Those places stand out
> in my mind like holy places.

And then I thought of that William Stafford poem:

> Freedom is not following a river.
> Freedom is following a river,
>   though, if you want to.

And then I thought of that Langston Hughes poem:

> Did you ever go down to the river—
> Two a.m. midnight by your self?
> Sit down by the river
> And wonder what you got left?

And I wept there, barefoot on the bank, in that holy place where water comes together with other water.

What I'm trying to tell you is that—at first—my walks did not involve birds. At first, my walks were about getting to the water, walking along the water, sometimes walking *in* the water, then walking home from the water. And I loved those water walks. Seeing and hearing the water had a healing effect. And even when I wasn't so focused on the creek, or on the neighborhood ponds, I still loved being outside, seemingly away from all the hard things.

But soon I realized that, when things were particularly rough—when my anxieties were riding high—even my water walks were not enough to clear my head. Instead, my walks would be overrun by all the racing thoughts that I was trying to walk away from.

On those mornings, when the hard things were particularly hard and the water wasn't enough to wash them away, I would look for George. Because George was my friend—and seeing George helped to quiet my mind.

I first saw George at the edge of one of our neighborhood ponds. I was crossing the bridge over the main pond and there he stood, perfectly still, head cocked to one side, staring intently at the water. I could tell he was watching something. Then he stabbed his face into the water and came up with—a fish! It was breathtaking.

Birders talk about having a "spark bird." Your spark bird is your origin story—your first encounter with that special bird that sparked your interest in ornithology. I once heard an Australian ornithologist talk about the time when, as a 10-year-old boy, he saw an Osprey take a fish from a lake, not more than 10 yards from where he was sitting. That Osprey was his spark bird.

In my neighborhood, we don't see Osprey, but we often see herons or egrets on the main pond (the one with the bridge, and the covered picnic tables).

At first, whenever I saw a Great Blue Heron in our neighborhood, I thought it was the same bird. I assumed that it lived in the woods nearby and that the pond served as its local diner. So I named this Great Blue Heron "George." And I started looking for George whenever I went for my walk. Sometimes I saw George down on the creek, but most of the time he was at the main pond. And watching George, as he fished on the bank, was soothing. Peaceful. *Helpful.* Looking for George—and then watching him for some time, after I found him—gave me something to focus on. Something to occupy my mind—to interrupt and displace the racing thoughts that otherwise threatened to overrun my walking.

For these reasons, I really liked seeing George. Of course, I now know that I'm not seeing the same bird every time. It turns out there are a lot of Great Blue Herons in this area. Once, when I was out walking with our youngest child, Ruby, we saw a siege of seven Great Blue Herons flying low overhead, like a formation of bombers. But I still call all of them "George."

As great as George is, though, I must tell you that George was not my spark bird. After seeing George, I kept going for walks every morning—to the creek and around the pond. But I wasn't looking for birds, because seeing George hadn't sparked any special interest in birds. The only bird I was ever looking for was George.

So what sparked my interest in birds and birding? Well, I've always liked owls. As a kid, I liked the owl in *Winnie-the-Pooh*. And I liked the owl in *The Secret of NIMH*. I guess you could say I liked cartoon owls. And I liked the little owl figurines that you could find in gift shops. I remember having a little owl that had been carved from white quartz, sitting on my dresser next to a few stray baseball cards and a wad of paper-route money. But as a kid, I liked owls only in a generic sort of way. I didn't know a Barn from a Barred, or a Spotted from a Screech. I remember one day when we filed into our middle-school cafeteria for a "Birds of Prey" demonstration, where a guy with a leather glove held an owl on his wrist and showed us how its head could turn *all the way around*. But other than that, I never saw an owl in real life. So no, an owl was not my spark bird.

I also always liked ducks. I grew up in Oregon, where I attended the University of Oregon my freshman year—so I'm a big Oregon Ducks fan. And we had pet ducks when I was in kindergarten: I remember holding the downy ducklings carefully, like delicate, dissembling tennis balls. But other than "Mallard," I couldn't tell you the name of any duck species. So no, a duck was not my spark bird, either.

My spark bird was the Pileated Woodpecker. But before I tell you about the woodpecker, I have to tell you about a board game. Because that's how it went for me: first there was George, then there was this board game, and *then* came the woodpecker.

After the world shut down in response to the COVID pandemic, our family—like many other families—started playing more board games. I've always liked board games, and we had some good ones stored in the bottom half of the giant armoire that sits in our living room. But during the pandemic, we had reason to expand our repertoire. So I bought some new board games. And one of the new games that I bought was called Wingspan.

Wingspan is a game about birds. But I didn't buy it because I was into birds—because I wasn't. Instead, I bought Wingspan because it looked like a moderately complex, interesting board game—and because the artwork was amazing. (The artwork *is* amazing: it's won awards for its amazingness.) So I bought Wingspan, and our family played it, and it quickly became one of my favorite games—partly because of the artwork and partly because of the gameplay itself, which is layered and complex, and more leisurely than competitive. I don't mean for this to sound too much like an advertisement—but if you like good (and beautiful) board games, I recommend Wingspan.

(If you want another good game with beautiful artwork, I recommend Arboretum, which is a card game about trees. I get no compensation for saying this.)

Anyway, I was taking walks through our neighborhood nearly every day, watching for George, and our family was playing lots of board games—including Wingspan—and it was good. The walks and the extra family time were helping when it came to handling the hard things.

But then June came, and some particularly hard things happened involving our second-eldest child, Mae. And then more hard things happened in August and September.

In late September, I went to Oregon—partly to cope with some of the hard things, and partly to check on my parents. It was wonderful to be back home, among the evergreens. And while I was there, I continued to go walking almost every morning. My parents still live in the Willamette Valley, on the hillside where I grew up, about three miles outside a little town called Monmouth. And on some mornings, I walked down the half-mile-long driveway and along the country road for a mile or so, and back again. Other mornings, I drove to the neighboring town of Independence, to Riverview Park, where I could walk along the Willamette River and look for George.

One morning, instead of driving to the river or walking down the driveway, I walked *up* the driveway to the back pasture. My parents live on 10 acres—two five-acre parcels that can be loosely described as the "main parcel," where the house is, and the "back pasture," which is up the hill a bit and separated from the house by trees (mostly fir, oak, and wild cherry). The back pasture was once an apple orchard, but it was cleared years ago. Now, it's mostly an open hillside with a few stray oaks and firs and a few leftover apple trees, gone feral. That morning, I wandered the back pasture, then sat on a fallen oak tree for a while, feeling pensive and nostalgic, as I looked out over the valley where I had grown up.

As I stood and started back toward the driveway, I heard a familiar cackling—a forest noise that I had heard many times throughout my childhood. As a kid, I had once imagined it was monkey chatter. But now—being old enough to know that monkeys don't live in Oregon—it sounded more like an angry squirrel. I had reached the tree line, where a lone leftover apple tree stood in front of some firs. And just after I heard this cackle, a large bird swooped down from one of the tall firs onto the squat apple tree. The bird was as big as a crow—mostly black, with some white marks on its face and neck, and a shock of red shooting out the back of its head like a punk rocker's mohawk. I froze, not wanting to scare it off. And I watched as the bird hacked at an overripe apple.

In all my years growing up on this hillside, running through these woods, I had never seen this bird before. I had heard its cackle many times, but I had never known—until now—that the cackle was a *bird*. It cackled again and lifted from the apple tree, back to the firs. I followed it, as best I could. And it was only when it returned to the trunk of a fir tree that I recognized it as a woodpecker by the way it perched vertically on the trunk, using its tail for leverage. I fumbled to take a quick photo with my phone. Then I named this new bird Frankie.

When I got back to my parents' house, I started searching the internet. I had to know what kind of bird Frankie was. When I found it, I showed my parents: the Pileated Woodpecker. The largest woodpecker in North America. Its name comes from Latin (*pileatus*) and is pronounced *PILL-ee-ay-tid* (though some say *PIE-lee-ay-tid*, and at least one source said *PIE-lay-tid*). It means "capped." I played a recording of its call, and my parents and I marveled that we had heard this bird in the woods so many times, for decades, yet none of us had ever caught sight of one until now. Later that same afternoon, with my brothers and their wives present—as we all sat (socially distanced) on the back deck—Frankie flew up to one of the giant firs that overshadows my parents' house and hung out there for a while, hopping from tree to tree nearby, as though wanting us to get a good look at him, now that we all knew he existed.

It was marvelous. That night in bed I kept marveling over it. How was I—a 48-year-old man—only just now seeing this bird? I had heard that sound in the woods so many times, for so many years—how did I not know that it was a bird? And it was so beautiful! I was so thrilled to know that it existed! How did I not know, until now, that it existed?

As I marveled, it occurred to me that, for the past several years, as a 40-something-year-old husband and father struggling through the hard things, I had stumbled into many moments like this. Moments of personal revelation: a realization about something from my childhood—or from my environment—that I had previously failed to recognize or to identify. These revelatory moments had always been illuminating, making life a little brighter. Clearer. Not necessarily easier. But *better*.

For example, all my life I've struggled with self-sabotage. I don't mean the typical fear of failure—the way we all sometimes give up on something because it feels safer to give up than to try and then fail. I do that sometimes, too. But here I'm talking about the sort of self-sabotage that happens even when I *know* I'm capable of succeeding. Sometimes I'm not afraid of failure *at all*, yet nevertheless I will do something to prevent my success. I'll make an excuse to avoid an important meeting. I'll sluff and fumble an important presentation. And internally I know that it has nothing to do with a fear of failure. So what's happening?

For a long time, I berated myself for this behavior. *You idiot! Why did you tank that presentation? You dolt! Why did you skip that meeting? Why are you like this?*

I know, I know: you're wondering what in the world all this has to do with the Pileated Woodpecker. I'm getting there.

One day, as I was telling my therapist about my childhood, the pieces clicked, and I suddenly realized why I'm like this. Throughout my early childhood—up through sixth grade—I received all kinds of positive reinforcement for being smart and academically successful. It was a huge part of my identity—a cornerstone of my sense of Self. I was, to myself and to others, The Kid Who Scored So High on That Test. So when my sixth-grade school counselor asked if I wanted to skip seventh grade, I felt like I was fulfilling my purpose in life. This kind of academic overachievement was Who I Am. *Of course* I wanted to skip seventh grade!

But that fall, when I showed up for eighth grade, I got a lot of side-eye from my new classmates. Some started calling me "the Brain"—and not in a fun-loving way. Others sneered at me for walking up to the high school for a 10th-grade biology class. ("You must not be that smart if you *want* to take harder classes.") I already felt out of place as the New Kid. And now suddenly my academic success, which had previously been a source of pride and self-worth, had become a mark of shame and the primary cause of my social alienation.

This polarized experience—being heavily praised for my academic success, then suddenly shunned for it—gave birth to some conflicting feelings about success. It's why I'm often confident in my ability to achieve it, but also often reluctant to achieve it. In my formative years, I learned that success brings praise—but that too much success brings rejection.

I ended up with a D in that 10th-grade biology class that I was taking as a new eighth grader. And I went on to graduate high school with a mediocre 3.2 GPA—not because the schoolwork was challenging, but because I deliberately skipped assignments and sluffed exams. I didn't recognize it at the time, but I was developing a habit of self-sabotage, hoping my more modest performance would reduce my sense of alienation.

And as I sat in my therapist's office and these pieces clicked together, I realized that—as an adult—I have continued to self-sabotage because I have continued to recycle my eighth-grade anxieties for the past 35 years.

As one does.

When I realized all this, it was like a light came on. Suddenly, so much of my life made more sense. I was so happy to finally see this thing that had always been there—this thing that I had always known was there, but that I was only just now seeing for what it truly was. Suddenly everything seemed brighter. Clearer. Not necessarily easier. But *better*.

It was the same sensation that I had felt when I discovered Frankie, the Pileated Woodpecker. I was so happy to finally see this thing that had always been there—this thing that I had always known was there, but that I was only just now seeing for what it truly was. It was like a light came on. When I saw Frankie and heard his cackle, the pieces clicked and the world seemed suddenly brighter. Clearer. *Better*.

And as I made these connections, lying in bed at my parents' house, the Pileated Woodpecker became—for me—a symbol of midlife enlightenment. A symbol for suddenly seeing clearly, for the first time, that which has been there all along. Such revelatory moments are golden moments. Moments that are crucial to life, to growth—and to surviving the hard things.

I returned to Texas a few days later, and my walks were different. Now I wanted to know the name of every bird that I saw. And I wanted to see all the birds that I hadn't been seeing. I wanted to have more golden moments like the moment I had had with Frankie.

So I walked out into the world, searching for birds.

The Ruby-crowned Kinglet
Corthylio calendula

It is more important to click with people
than to click the shutter.

– Alfred Eisenstaedt

The hero's journey begins with leaving the house. Odysseus left his house to fight a war in Troy. Dorothy left her house to set out on a yellow brick road. Huck Finn snuck out of a house and got into a canoe—then traded the canoe for a raft. Leopold Bloom left his house to go buy a pork kidney. Luke left his home on Tatooine to fight the Evil Empire. Bilbo Baggins threw a party, then left with some dwarves. The Prodigal Son left his home to make his own way in the world. Katniss Everdeen volunteered to serve as tribute. And Moana—like Huck—snuck out of her house and got into a boat.

Me? I walked out my front door and went looking for birds.

As I said, over the past few years, things hadn't been going so great. My wife's brother had been killed by a police officer; my wife had been struggling with PTSD and depression; I had been recovering from some addictive behavior—then I was diagnosed with prostate cancer; and we had just experienced some hard things involving our second-eldest child. Meanwhile, Collin County had just surpassed 100 deaths from the new coronavirus—and by the end of October we would hit 175. Our neighborhood elementary school had shut down and the high-school football team was in quarantine. By early November, the weekly number of cases was spiking. It had taken five months for Collin County to reach 100 deaths—but it would take less than three months to go from 100 to 200. And by the end of November, it would be 250.

My body was a tight coil of stress and anxiety. Work was just as busy as before—but my firm had cut salaries in response to the shutdown. The kids were facing uncertainties with school. And in late November we would get some traumatic news from our eldest son.

The hard things were piling up.

But this book isn't about the hard things—remember? This book is about the good things. The *healing* things. Those things that have helped me to survive the hard things.

After meeting Frankie in Oregon and returning to Texas, I bought a cheap pair of hiking boots. I dug some binoculars out of a coat closet. And I walked out my front door, headed for the neighborhood creek, looking for another revelation.

It would come in the form of the Ruby-Crowned Kinglet.

But before I tell you about the kinglet, I want to say a few words about starting out as a new birder. As a newbie, I knew I would need help with identifying the birds I was hoping to find. And now I feel like I can offer some recommendations—in case you're looking to begin a similar journey. If you're not interested in beginning a similar journey, that's okay—just bear with me. It'll only take a few paragraphs.

First, for bird identification, I recommend two apps for your phone: iBird PRO and Merlin Bird ID. The iBird PRO app has drawings and photos and lots of information about over 900 North American bird species, and it has a heavy-duty search tool that allows you to narrow your search by size, shape, primary color, secondary color, etc. I bought the "Birds Around Me" add-on, which I found helpful as a beginner. And I also bought the "Photo Sleuth" add-on, which allows you to upload a photo and then offers three possible identifications, using percentages to indicate levels of certainty. For example, for my blurry photo of a little brownish-grayish bird, it might suggest

Lincoln's Sparrow (44%), Song Sparrow (33%), Chipping Sparrow (23%). This means my photo is bad and the app is just humoring me. But with a better photo, it might say something like Lincoln's Sparrow (88%), Song Sparrow (8%), some other sparrow (4%). That's helpful.

The Merlin app likewise has a photo-ID tool, and the two apps can complement each other. While iBird has the benefit of providing percentages, Merlin has the benefit of limiting its suggestions to only those birds that exist where your photo was taken, at the time of year when it was taken. (For example: Collin County in the springtime.) If you upload the same photo to both apps, and both apps suggest the same bird, then that's probably your bird.

And the Merlin app can also identify birds by *sound*, which is a game-changer. Many birds are hard to identify by sight alone—especially from a distance. (See sparrows and flycatchers.) But if the bird is making noise, Merlin can help you figure out what you're hearing. And of course, the name of the app is brilliant: a nifty pun on Merlin the bird (a small falcon) and Merlin the magician (because the app works like magic).

Second, for list-keeping, I recommend eBird. Merlin and eBird are both produced by the Cornell Lab of Ornithology, and they are linked. If you create an eBird account online, and then use that account to log in to both apps, your eBird lists will be available to (and reviewed by) ornithologists at the Cornell Lab—so every time you go birding and create a list on eBird, you'll be contributing to science. And your "Life List" of all the bird species you've seen will show up in Merlin. The eBird app also has an excellent "explore" tool that will show you birding hotspots on a map—with info about the birds you are likely to see, and the birds that have recently been seen in that spot, according to the lists submitted by other birders. This is an incredibly useful tool when you're new to birding—or when you're a seasoned birder but you're new to the area and need to find a good place to go for a walk.

As for books, if you want a paginated bird guide to supplement the apps on your phone, I recommend *The Sibley Guide to Birds*. The art in Sibley's guide is beautiful—and helpful—and every page is packed with useful information. But Sibley's Guide is hefty. So for a "pocket guide," I suggest Stan Tekiela's *Birds of* series. I have his *Birds of Texas* and his *Birds of Oregon*, and they're pretty handy.

Besides books and apps, you'll also want footwear that can get wet or muddy. And you'll want some binoculars, or a scope, or a camera with a big zoom lens—something to help you get a closer look at all those birds. (A lot of them are small!) I don't have any special recommendations for cameras or binoculars. Just find something in a price range that works for you. I have $35 binoculars that work great. And sometimes I borrow my wife's camera, with its 300mm lens.

And this brings me back to the Ruby-crowned Kinglet. Like hummingbirds, the kinglets (both the Ruby-crowned Kinglet and the Golden-crowned Kinglet) are among the smallest birds we get in North America. They're tiny (3")—and they're always moving. They're known for their pendulous, sac-like nests, which are elaborately decorated with lichen and moss, and held together with stolen spider webs. But we don't see their nests here in Texas because the kinglets spend nesting season mostly in Canada. They come south to Texas only for fall and winter.

It was early October when I returned to Texas, after meeting Frankie—but it didn't feel much like fall. In Oregon, the morning air had been crisp: I had worn jeans, a sweatshirt or jacket, and a tuque on every walk. In contrast, in Texas it was still in the 80s. So I was back in shorts and a t-shirt. But in the northern places like Oregon, the temperatures were dropping—sending birds southward, to Texas.

After a few walks through the neighborhood with my binoculars, I realized it might be better to use my wife's camera—with its zoom lens—to help me with bird-identification. I was catching only brief glimpses of birds in the bushes and trees—

and for some reason they wouldn't hold still while I stood there on the trail, trying to look them up on an app. I needed to take advantage of those photo-ID tools. So I started taking photos. And I quickly learned that, if I set the camera to rapid-fire, I could snap 20–30 photos of a little bird that was darting from branch to branch. And—if I was lucky—I might end up with two or three photos that actually had the bird in them, in good-enough focus for a possible ID.

And isn't this what photography is for? Freezing already-past moments for future use? Eudora Welty said, "A good snap-shot keeps a moment from running away." This was my intent: to snap a shot of the bird I was seeing before it could fly away. And I figured this would also improve my identification skills: as I identified more birds using photos, eventually I wouldn't need the camera—I would be able to identify what I was seeing without having to freeze it for later. In Dorothea Lange's words: "The camera is an instrument that teaches people how to see without a camera."

By the way, I've also always liked what Andy Warhol said: "The best thing about a picture is that it never changes, even when the people in it do." Photos can be an effort to contain or control what cannot be contained or controlled. Time. People. Nature. Life. Change.

Now I should mention that, for months—in my effort to deal with the hard things—I had been trying to learn more about mindfulness. I had learned that mindfulness, as a con-cept, helped to explain why my walks could be so peaceful—why looking for George, and watching him catch fish, could be so calming. This activity focused my mind on the *present*, on what I was experiencing in the moment, through my five sens-es—and this focus on the present provided a respite from all the past pains and future worries that plagued my mind throughout the rest of the day. By October, I had become fairly sure that I fully grasped this concept—and I felt pretty confident that I was "doing the mindfulness thing" whenever I went walking.

But then one day—as I was walking near the main pond in our neighborhood—I saw three tiny birds, flitting among the half-bare branches of an oak tree, not more than 10 feet away. I knew I was seeing something new, and I got excited. I raised the camera and tried taking photos—but the birds were moving too fast. They kept darting from branch to branch, and neither my autofocus nor my manual focus could keep up. I grew frustrated. I stood there for what felt like an hour (it was a minute, at most), trying—and failing—to digitally capture these little birds so that I could figure out later what they were. And then they flew away—too far for photos. They had been *right there*, and I had missed them completely. I had seen nothing but blurred movement through an unfocused lens. I wanted to throw the camera into the pond.

I continued my walk, but it was no longer peaceful. I was too distraught over missing the moment.

Then, a few days later, I saw the same little birds in the same oak tree by the pond. I recognized them by their hyperactivity. And this time I didn't bother with the camera. I surrendered. I let it go, knowing it would be pointless. Instead, I just watched the birds with my bare eyes. Again, they were just 10 feet away. I inched closer, feeling my toes flex as I leaned forward. I listened to the birds' busy mutterings—*je-dit, je-dit, je-dit*—as they moved about, never stopping for more than a second. I noted their olive color, their little teardrop shape, their white wing bars. I even saw a tiny fleck of red on the top of one's head, before it moved again. I realized I was holding my breath, and I rocked back on my heels and inhaled deeply, savoring the moment. Then—one by one—the little birds flew away.

I didn't get any photos. But this time I had seen the little birds clearly enough to look them up, and to identify them as a small court of Ruby-crowned Kinglets. It was the most fulfilling walk I had taken since returning from Oregon.

And this is how I learned what it meant to really be *present*. So often—even when we think we're focusing on the present—we're trying so hard to capture or control what is happening that we miss what is happening. We all know that person who is so busy taking photos of the party or the meal or the moment that they aren't really participating in the party or the meal or the moment. Maybe sometimes that person is you? I know for sure that the first time I saw the kinglets, that person was me.

The kinglet taught me to stop trying to contain what I cannot contain. To stop trying to freeze those already-past moments for future scrutiny. To tune in to my five senses. To tune in to what is happening right now, right here in front of me. I've learned that, if I do this, I will see
so many things
so much more clearly.

The Tufted Titmouse

Baeolophus bicolor

> You are supposed to stay still. It won't
> always save you, but sometimes it will.
>
> – William Stafford

We live in a neighborhood called Whitley Place, which reposes on the east end of a town called Prosper. If you look at a map, Whitley Place is roughly rectangular, boxed by roads on three sides: Prosper Trail to the north, 1st Street to the south, and Custer Road to the east. To the west is some farmland that, as of this writing, remains mostly undeveloped—land that stretches from Whitley Place to a reservoir called Town Lake.

Custer Road is not only the eastern boundary of Whitley Place, but also the eastern boundary of Prosper, separating Prosper from McKinney. And to the south is Frisco. You might have heard that Frisco and McKinney are two of the fastest growing suburban cities in the country—both have been spotlighted in glossy magazines as being among America's "best places to live." When we moved to Prosper in 2013, it felt like a small farming town. The population sign said just over 12,000. But now, the population sign says just over 35,000—and they're expanding both Custer Road and Prosper Trail from two lanes to four, as they build another new high school on 1st Street.

Whitley Place is where I started taking my morning walks, just after the world shut down. It's a nice neighborhood. Wilson Creek cuts through it, running from the northwest corner to the southeast corner. And we live in the northeast corner, near the elementary school. If you head southwest from our house, through the neighborhood, you'll cross a bridge over the creek that separates one side of the neighborhood from the other. And right after the bridge, there's a small pond on the left (with a fountain) and the big main pond on the right (with a footbridge and some covered picnic tables). There's also a paved path that runs along the creek and past the two ponds, and out to a third pond that sits by Custer Road by the southeast entrance to the neighborhood. Our kids call the third pond the "circle pond" because the paved path loops all the way around it, in a circle.

When I returned from Oregon and turned my morning walks through Whitley Place into birding expeditions, I started learning more about identifying bird species. And as I was learning more about identifying bird species, I had to refresh my 10th-grade knowledge of biological taxonomy. The taxonomic structure looks like this:

> Class – *Aves* (all birds)
> Order – e.g., *Passeriformes* (perching birds)
> Family – e.g., *Paridae* (chickadees, titmouses, etc.)
> Genus – e.g., *Poecile* (chickadees)
> Species – e.g., *Poecile carolinensis* (Carolina Chickadee)

In the bird world there are lots of orders, and each order may contain multiple families, and each family may contain multiple genera (the plural form of "genus"), and each genus may contain multiple species. And the goal for a birder is to identify individual species. It's not enough to say, "That's a chickadee." You want to be able to distinguish a Black-capped Chickadee from a Carolina Chickadee.

(A quick note about capitalization: there's a debate among bird grammarians over whether bird names should be capitalized—i.e., should it be "Black-capped Chickadee" or "blackcapped chickadee"? Personally, I side with those who think the name of a family or genus—such as "chickadee" or "woodpecker"—is like the generic noun "car" or "truck." But the name of a specific species is more like the proper name of a specific automobile—meaning "Black-capped Chickadee" is like "Toyota Camry." So throughout this book I capitalize the names of specific species like "Black-capped Chickadee," but not the names of broader groups like "chickadees.")

Before I started this journey, I knew about chickadees. That is, I knew that there were birds called "chickadees." I knew they were little birds with black-and-white heads, and I knew that they got their name from the sound they make (*chick-a-dee-dee-dee*). But that was pretty much all I knew. And I thought "chickadee" referred to just one kind of bird.

But I quickly discovered that in North America there are roughly seven different species of chickadee (depending on how you define "North America"). Here in Texas, we have the Carolina Chickadee, which is common throughout the South. But Oregon has the Black-capped Chickadee, the Chestnut-backed Chickadee, and—in the drier, eastern part of the state—the Mountain Chickadee. Meanwhile, up in Canada and Alaska, they have the Boreal Chickadee and the Gray-headed Chickadee. And I'll let you guess where you might find the Mexican Chickadee.

In the same family as the chickadees are the titmouses. It's tempting to use "titmice" as the plural form of "titmouse," but the suffix -*mouse* is unrelated to the word we use for the tiny rodent, and it shouldn't be pluralized in the same way. *Tit-* comes from a Scandinavian word meaning "little," and -*mouse* comes from an Old English word (*mase*) that also meant "little." So "titmouse" literally means "little little." I had never heard the word before I started birding. But North America has five different species of titmouse. Here in Collin County, we have the Tufted Titmouse, which—like the Carolina Chickadee—is fairly common throughout the South and up into the Midwest. The Black-crested Titmouse lives in Central and South Texas. The Juniper Titmouse lives in the desert states of Utah, Nevada, and Arizona. The Oak Titmouse lives mostly in California. And the

Bridled Titmouse lives mostly in Mexico—though its range also reaches up into parts of Arizona.

I first saw the Tufted Titmouse on a walk through Whitley Place—just a couple days before I watched those Ruby-crowned Kinglets with my bare eyes. And over the next couple weeks, I discovered something cool about the Tufted Titmouse: if you call out to them, they will respond. They're curious little birds with a lilting, flute-like call—usually a series of 3–5 whistles. People often ascribe two syllables to each whistle, representing it phonetically as *peter, peter, peter*. On many mornings, I would hear this call as I walked along the path, among the trees. And I discovered that, if you hear this call, and you know how to whistle, you can respond and the titmouse will exchange whistles with you, back and forth, for quite a long time. Sometimes the titmouse will even come closer, to investigate. And sometimes you can initiate the conversation yourself—you can call out (with your whistle), even before you've heard any titmouse, and after a few tries, you might just get a response.

When I first discovered the Tufted Titmouse's conversational tendencies, it reminded me of the "call and response" motif that is common in music, and in some folklore and literary traditions. The motif is common in both jazz and the blues, for example. In Led Zeppelin's version of the blues classic "You Shook Me," Robert Plant calls out with a high-pitched wail, and Jimmy Page responds—mimicking the high-pitched wail on his guitar—and the two go back and forth, between voice and guitar, calling and responding to each other. Children's songs and campfire songs often use a call-and-response structure, too. And of course many religious rituals have a scripted call-and-response (often in the form of questions and answers). Think of Catholicism's Catechism, or Judaism's Haggadah.

Most heroic journeys also begin with a call-and-response. Usually there's some kind of "call to adventure," to which the hero responds. Sometimes the response is a refusal, at first—or at least some show of reluctance. Think of Jonah running away to avoid God's call. Or the grisly old soldier (or spy) who doesn't want to get involved in stopping the latest plot to destroy the world because, for crying out loud, he's *retired*. But eventually, of course, the hero responds to the call. That's what makes them the hero. Heroes *respond*.

In Saskatchewan, there's an old tale—or myth—about a Cree warrior who was paddling his canoe through the night to get to the woman that he loved. As he paddled under the stars, listening to the sounds of the river, he heard a voice call his name. He stopped paddling and responded in his native tongue: "Who calls?" Then he repeated in French: "Qu'appelle?" But he heard nothing. He resumed paddling—but then, again, he heard a voice call his name. And he responded: "Who calls? Qu'appelle?" But then nothing. He resumed paddling and reached the home of his beloved at dawn. But her father met him outside to say that she had died in the night. Before she had died, said the father, she had whispered his name—two times. The Cree warrior fell to his knees, weeping. And legend has it that travelers on the Qu'Appelle River can still hear the echo of the Cree warrior's voice, as he calls out, "Qu'appelle?"— with no response.

I like this story because the layers are wonderful: there's a call, then the hero's response, which is itself a call (asking "Who calls?"), to which there is no response. Both characters call, but each receives no response. The story is tragic and haunting precisely for the absence of responses. And in a perfect, tragic twist, the legend transforms the heroic act—the warrior's response—into an act of responding *by calling*. In other words, yes, traditionally the hero *responds*. But the Cree story suggests that sometimes the hero *calls*.

I confess that I am not always good at asking for help when I need it. And sometimes, when I do ask, the trepidation that I've had to overcome prevents me from waiting patiently for what I've requested. After going to the trouble of asking, I'm quick to assume that the answer isn't coming. Or that it won't be what I was hoping for. So I give up and move on.

One particularly difficult morning—when I was feeling overweighted with hard things—I was having trouble focusing. I had been struggling with what to do, with how to handle some of the hard things. And even if I thought I might ask someone for help, I didn't know who to ask.

For my walk that morning, I wanted to get out of the neighborhood. I had just started to expand my horizons beyond Whitley Place by exploring a couple nearby parks. So that morning, I drove a few miles to Bonnie Wenk Park, where the light was still dim because the sun wasn't quite up yet.

As I started walking, I occasionally saw movement in the branches. But it seemed ghostlike, chimerical. I felt distracted, scattered—detached. I'd been walking for 15–20 minutes when I realized that I hadn't identified a single bird. I wasn't sure if I'd even *seen* a single bird—though I'm sure there were birds all around me, ready to be seen. I tried to identify what I'd been thinking about, but I couldn't pin down my thoughts. I couldn't even remember where I had walked, or how I had arrived at where I was.

I stopped and stared at a crack in the sidewalk. I took a deep breath. I whispered, "Heavenly Father," as though I might say a prayer—but I couldn't put any words together. I noted the anxiety constricting my chest, twisting like a rope in my stomach. And my impulse was to start walking faster. To *run*. I considered sprinting across the grass—maybe running sprints back and forth to work off the jittery tightness I was feeling. But then I saw another movement in the trees and, without thinking, I whistled my best imitation of a Tufted Titmouse.

Nothing happened. But instead of moving on, I stood still. I whistled again. And I listened. Then I whistled again. And I listened. Then again. And I listened. And I realized that the whistling—and the listening—had given me something to focus on. It had quieted my mind. I felt myself breathe, in and out, and my chest opened up. I whistled again. And I listened again.

And as I breathed, in and out, I felt the rope in my stomach unravel. I whistled again. And I listened again.

And then it came: a response from high in the trees. *Peter, peter, peter.* I whistled again. And I got another response. I couldn't see it at first, but the bird and I exchanged whistles until I caught a flutter in the corner of my eye. Most of the lower leaves had fallen. And there—at eye level, in the wiry underbrush—was a Tufted Titmouse. But this wasn't the bird that was still answering my whistle from high above. So I kept whistling. And a moment later, a second titmouse fluttered down. Then another. And another! And I stood there—still whistling— as a flute of five titmouses assembled in the underbrush, exchanging friendly whistles with me as the sun came up. Like the answer to a prayer.

We all want someone to respond when we need help. But first we have to call for it. And then we have to be still, and wait for it. The calling and the waiting are every bit as important as the response. When the response doesn't come, it can be heartbreaking; and when it does come, it can be glorious. But the response isn't everything. The calling itself is a heroic act. And the waiting is part of the hero's call. The waiting—the being still, the stillness of waiting—opens us up. It prepares us, *enables* us to receive the response.

The Blue-headed Vireo

Vireo solitarius

If I am not what you say I am,
then you are not who you think you are.

– James Baldwin

I mentioned that, by November, I had started venturing to other locations outside our neighborhood. The first place I went was Bonnie Wenk Park—a sprawling collection of open fields, sports fields, and playgrounds, with patches of dense trees, creeks, a large pond, and a marshy area near one of the playgrounds. It's where I first saw the Red-shouldered Hawk, the Hooded Merganser, and the Cedar Waxwing. (I'll tell you more about those birds later.) But the sports fields are crowded on the weekends—so I recommend that you go on a weekday, when the park isn't teeming with screaming kids and parents.

I also soon discovered Town Lake Park, and Erwin Park, and Nora Haney Park. All these parks—including Bonnie Wenk— are here in Collin County, within five miles of my house. And each provides a slightly different environment with a slightly different mix of birds. At Town Lake I saw Ring-necked Ducks and Northern Shovelers. At Erwin Park I saw the Hermit Thrush and Harris's Sparrow. At Nora Haney I saw the Gadwall and the Bufflehead. By the end of November—after just two months of birding—I had seen over 70 different species.

And I was feeling calmer, happier. *Better.*

But I was still a beginning birder. I was eager to add new species to my Life List, but unsure about my bird-identification skills. Sometimes I would fret about adding a new bird to my list because I wasn't sure whether I'd really seen what I thought I had seen. And sometimes I would confidently add a new bird only to go back and remove it later, after the excitement had subsided and I could assess my confidence more soberly.

In his book *Zen Birding*, David White tells a story about meeting a guy named Sam while birding one day along the Connecticut River. White had his binoculars on a flock of Red-winged Blackbirds when he was approached by Sam, who said: "So you're a birdwatcher, eh?" White nodded and Sam said, "I gave it a try, back when I was in college. But I got bored with it. I saw six hundred and something species in the first year, and figured, what do you do after that?"

White was understandably impressed. At the time of this encounter, White had been birding for over 10 years and his Life List was "quite a bit short of six hundred." He expressed his admiration for Sam's accomplishment. And Sam asked if he could take a look through White's binoculars.

White obliged. And when Sam looked out at the flock of Red-winged Blackbirds, he said: "Tricolored Blackbirds. Yep. They've always been one of my favorites."

After a pause, White asked casually, "Have you done much birding in California?" And when Sam said he hadn't, White surmised that Sam's impressive Life List was probably mostly a product of Sam's imagination. The Tricolored Blackbird is relatively rare. It exists only in California (and on the Baja California Peninsula)—and even there it is greatly outnumbered by the similar-looking Red-winged Blackbird, which is common throughout North America. In other words, Sam had just glibly misidentified a flock of Red-winged Blackbirds, without even realizing that he was 3,000 miles out of range for seeing the Tricolored Blackbird.

Sam's mistake represents one of two types of mistakes that a birder can make. One type is mistaking a commoner (the Red-winged Blackbird) for a rarity (the Tricolored Blackbird). And the other is mistaking a rarity for a commoner, which often happens when you're not really paying attention—especially during migration, when birds that are rare for your area are passing through. Each type of misidentification involves an assumption. In *Zen Birding*, White suggests that the first type of misidentification (mistaking a commoner for a rarity) involves an *optimistic* assumption—that you're seeing something more special than what you're actually seeing. And the second type (mistaking a rarity for a commoner) involves a *pessimistic* assumption—that you're seeing the same old thing you always see, when in fact you're seeing something special. The optimist might have a desire to feel important, while the pessimist might have a fear of being wrong or of appearing boastful.

I have no idea which mistake is more frequent among birders. But it's interesting to think about which mistake I might be more likely to make myself, on any given day.

After reading White's story about Sam, I started feeling even more insecure about my growing Life List. How many birds had I misidentified? (And why?) So I went back through my list and deleted a few birds that I wasn't feeling confident about.

Now let me tell you about the Blue-headed Vireo. Like warblers, vireos are singers, but they have thicker bills, are less colorful, and—as far as I can tell—they are less popular and less widely loved. (In my early assessment, warblers seem to be the darlings of the birder world.) Despite this second-class status, the Red-eyed Vireo is known as the most prodigious singer in North America. The naturalist Louise de Kiriline Lawrence once recorded a single Red-eyed Vireo vocalizing 22,197 times with 40 song variations during just 10 of the 14 hours of daylight in a single day. (Imagine all those tallies in her notebook.)

Both the Red-eyed Vireo and the White-eyed Vireo are fairly common in North Texas in the summertime. The White-eyed Vireo really does have white eyes, with a tiny black pupil—and the Red-eyed Vireo really does have red eyes, with a tiny black pupil. But vireos are small, and their eyes are even smaller, so you can't readily identify them by the color of their eyes. Instead, both birds are more readily identified by their eyebrows. The White-eyed Vireo has a yellow eyebrow (almost unique among vireos found in Texas). And the Red-eyed Vireo has a sharply distinct, long white eyebrow. But I learned all this much later. I didn't see either of these birds when I started birding in October, because both had already flown south for the winter.

Less common—but still present in North Texas throughout the summertime—are the Warbling Vireo, the Yellow-throated Vireo, and Bell's Vireo. The Warbling Vireo has a white eyebrow that is not nearly as distinct as the Red-eyed Vireo's. And the Yellow-throated Vireo has a small yellow eyebrow, like the White-eyed Vireo—but the name of the Yellow-throated Vireo tells you what distinguishes it from the others. As for Bell's Vireo, I think it is the drabbest, most generic looking vireo in North Texas—and I usually identify it as the vireo that doesn't have any of the distinctive features that the others have. But again, I didn't learn any of this until much later because these vireos had all flown south by the time October and November rolled around.

Then there's the Philadelphia Vireo and the Blue-headed Vireo, both of which summer mostly in Canada and winter along the Gulf Coast and farther southward, into Mexico. These two vireos pass through North Texas only during migration. Like the other vireos I've mentioned, the Philadelphia Vireo (which closely resembles the Warbling Vireo) heads south around September. But the Blue-headed Vireo doesn't travel as far south as the others—and it passes through North Texas much later than the others. Which is why I was able to see a Blue-headed Vireo in November.

In my admittedly limited experience, it's relatively rare to spot a Blue-headed Vireo in Collin County. They pass through only twice a year. And they tend to stay high in the canopy—moving from branch to branch as they forage for insects among the leaves—making them even harder to see.

For me, it's hard to pick a favorite bird in the same way that it's hard to pick a favorite book or a favorite song. But the Blue-headed Vireo is possibly my favorite bird. I think they're beautiful. Part of it might be the bold white spectacles. (I, too, wear glasses.) And I probably love them, in part, because they're so hard to find. Throughout my first year of birding, I saw the Blue-headed Vireo just three times—twice in November and just once the following spring. And I never got a very good look at it.

In fact, the first time I saw the Blue-headed Vireo, I thought it was a Ruby-crowned Kinglet. The behavior was similar: a small, mostly olive-colored passerine moving quickly from branch to branch, looking for bugs. When I saw its movement, it was too far away for me to see the bird clearly with my naked eyes. And through the camera, I could barely keep the bird in focus or in frame, as I tried to follow it from branch to branch. So I just snapped a few photos and assumed it was the kinglet— a bird that, by November, I had seen many times and felt confident about identifying.

It was only later, as I was going through my photos, that I saw the bird's bold, stark-white spectacles and realized that I had seen something new. Something different and rare. I was excited to add a new bird to my Life List. But I was also disappointed that, instead of cherishing the moment and pursuing a better look, I had turned away thinking it was something I had already seen.

As humans, we make assumptions. We rely on prior perceptions, preconceived notions, built-in biases. This can be useful. Helpful. Perhaps even necessary. Our brains rely on preestablished patterns to help us make sense of the world.

But sometimes assumptions are harmful. Sometimes we're too hasty in identifying what we see because we think we already know what we're looking at. And as a result, we misjudge things. Assumptions are what give us illusions. In our assumptions, we fail to see what is really happening. We fail to see people for who they really are. And sometimes this creates—or exacerbates—the hard things that we suffer in life.

I love the Blue-headed Vireo not just for its spectacles and not only because it is harder to find, but also because—when I found it—I did not realize at first that I had found it. I love the Blue-headed Vireo because it reminds me that things are not always what they appear to be. The Blue-headed Vireo reminds me to question my assumptions. It reminds me that, if we do not take time to look again, and again—more closely—we will never really see what is rare and special about the present moment, about this current experience, or about the particular person who is standing right there in front of us.

The Great Horned Owl
Bubo virginianus

> Where danger is,
> there grows the saving power also.
>
> – Hölderlin

There's this scene in *The Secret of NIMH* that I still remember from when I watched the movie as a kid. The movie is about Mrs. Brisby, a widowed field mouse (voiced by Elizabeth Hartman) who must move her family before the farmer starts plowing his field. But she can't move her son, Timothy, because he has pneumonia. So she doesn't know what to do. She befriends a clumsy crow named Jeremy (voiced by Dom DeLouise) and—on a neighbor's recommendation—she goes to visit the Great Owl for advice. This visit to the Great Owl is the scene I'm talking about—the scene from a 1982 animated movie that I still remember so vividly.

I remember the scene so vividly because it scared the crap out of me. Mrs. Brisby herself is deathly afraid to visit the Great Owl. She's a mouse, and she says several times: "Owls eat mice." When she and Jeremy arrive at the Great Owl's old hollow tree, it is like a haunted house—dark and musty, filled with cobwebs and clattering piles of mouse bones. The Great Owl is an imposing giant with fiery red eyes, fierce talons, and a booming voice (provided by John Carradine, who was known best for playing Count Dracula in old horror movies).

Mrs. Brisby is deathly afraid to face the Great Owl. But she edges past the clattering piles of mouse bones, into the dark hollow tree, because facing the Great Owl is *necessary*. It is terrifying—even life-threatening. But it is the only chance Mrs. Brisby has at salvation.

I told you about how, when I was a kid, I used to have a little owl figurine, carved from a chunk of translucent white stone, sitting on my dresser next to a few stray baseball cards and some wadded-up paper-route money. I wish I still had that little owl figurine.

As a new birder, I quickly learned that owls are not related to hawks and eagles. You would think that all the birds of prey would be closely related—but it turns out that hawks, owls, and falcons aren't even in the same biological order, let alone the same family.

Hawks and eagles are related—in the order *Accipitriformes*, which also includes kites and vultures. I'll tell you more about the accipiters later, in the chapter about the Osprey.

Falcons have their own order, *Falconiformes*. I don't have much to say about the falcons in this book. But did you know that the kestrel (a falcon) was once known as the "windfucker"? This wasn't a nasty slang nickname. This was the bird's common colloquial name—the way "yellowhammer" is a common colloquial name for the Northern Flicker (a species of woodpecker). Or the way the Yellow-rumped Warbler is known in some parts as the "butterbutt." Back in 15th- to 16th-century Britain, the Anglo-Saxon verb *fucking* was considered low-brow, but it wasn't as offensive or controversial as it is in 21st-century America. It was generally considered a euphemism for "beating." (Which is perhaps why the word still has brutish connotations when used in reference to sex.) The kestrel was known for its ability to hover in midair, beating its wings against the wind while keeping its head perfectly still, as it searched for prey in the grass below. Hence: it was known as the windfucker. Here in America, among a handful of other falcons, we have the American Kestrel. Next time you see one, you can decide for yourself what to call it. And that's all I'll say about falcons.

Owls have their own order, *Strigiformes*, which comprises just two families: *Strigidae* and *Tytonidae*. Apparently, the family *Tytonidae* is devoted entirely to barn owls—including the Barn Owl, which is the only barn owl that lives here in North America. Technically, it's called the American Barn Owl to distinguish it from other barn owls (like the Eastern Barn Owl or the Common Barn Owl). But here in America we just call it the Barn Owl because it's the only barn owl we have.

The other owl family, *Strigidae*, includes all the other owl species that you've probably heard of—like the Snowy Owl, the Screech-Owl (Eastern, Western, and Pacific versions), the Spotted Owl, and the Great Horned Owl. (Yes, there is also a Lesser Horned Owl—but it lives in South America.) And then there are some owls that you might not have heard of, like the Barred Owl, the Short-eared Owl, the Long-eared Owl, the Burrowing Owl, the Northern Saw-whet Owl, and the Great Gray Owl—which is the world's largest owl, standing over two feet tall with a more-than-four-foot wingspan. The Great Gray Owl lives in Alaska and Canada, in the higher Rocky Mountains, and in Minnesota and northern Wisconsin. If you've seen that movie, *The Big Year*, the Great Gray Owl is the owl that Jack Black's character sees in the woods with his dad.

Oh, and while I'm at it, I must mention that there is an owl endemic to the Solomon Islands called the Fearful Owl. This is obviously the best bird name ever, and—based on the name alone—I will probably have to plan a trip to the Solomon Islands sometime soon.

In all seriousness, I would really like to see more owls. But until I do more birding at night—or at least during those dim hours just before dawn, or just after dusk—I'm not likely to see very many owls.

The Great Horned Owl can hear a mouse rustling in leaves from 300 yards away. Imagine that. Imagine you are standing at one end of a football field, and you can hear a mouse in the leaves—not at the other end of the football field, but *three foot-*

ball fields away. And the Great Horned Owl is a fearsome predator. It doesn't just kill mice. It kills squirrels and rabbits. And it has been known to kill skunks, raccoons, porcupines—even hawks and other raptors. The ends of its feathers are ragged, making its flight silent, so that it can swoop in and attack unannounced.

Owls have been considered harbingers of doom for centuries. Lillith, the Sumerian goddess of the underworld, is usually depicted with wings and talons, and accompanied by two owls. The Roman statesman, Pliny, wrote that owls foretell "nothing but evil" and are to be "dreaded more than any other bird." The Aztecs associated the owl with the god of the dead. And in many ancient cultures, the call of an owl signaled the coming of death. In ancient China, some believed that owls snatched away the soul.

On the other hand, owls have also been associated with wisdom, learning, and prophecy. In the legends of King Arthur, Merlin is often portrayed with an owl on his shoulder. Some Australian tribes believed that when the tribe's medicine man died, his soul became an owl. Some North American tribes believed that eating an owl's eye would restore your eyesight or help you to see at night. In French folklore, if a pregnant woman heard an owl call, she knew she would be having a girl.

I am fascinated by this conflicting combination of wisdom and doom. And again, it makes me wish that I still had that little owl figurine, carved from stone.

In *The Secret of NIMH*, the Great Owl embodies this conflicting combination of wisdom and doom. He holds the answers that Mrs. Brisby seeks—but he also threatens the death that she fears. When she musters the courage to face the Great Owl, she walks out from the shadows—exposes herself—and risks a horrifying end. But the Great Owl doesn't kill her. Instead, he gives her what she needs. Then his great wings unfurl, and he lifts from the old hollow tree and flies away.

***

If you go to counseling, if you read self-help books, if you participate in a 12-step program—if you do anything aimed at self-improvement—everyone everywhere will tell you that you have to open yourself up. *Vulnerability* is key. You have to let others see the whole you, warts and all. To improve your marriage or other relationships. To improve your sense of self-worth. To live an authentic life. To accomplish real change. To heal wounds and to recover from the past. To gain all of this, or any of this, you must be willing to expose yourself—and to risk the possible losses that may come with exposure.

One night, around 11:00 p.m., I heard hooting outside our window. I could tell it was a Great Horned Owl, with its distinct *hoot h-hooooo, hooo hooo*. The call was loud—as though the owl was perched right over our bedroom. (The Great Horned Owl's sonorous hoot can be heard from 150–200 yards away.) I went to the back door and opened it quietly—but it was freezing outside. The cold air speared me in the chest. So I didn't go out. Instead I closed the door and just listened at the window. As a result, I didn't see anything.

A couple weeks later, just after midnight, I heard it again—just as loud. And this time there were two of them: a pair of owls, calling back and forth to each other. But—again—it was pitch-black and freezing outside. So—again—I just listened at the window and didn't see anything.

A few weeks later, I woke up to go to the bathroom at 3:00 a.m. and the owls were back. Two Great Horned Owls in casual conversation, seemingly right above our bedroom window. Yet again, it was freezing outside. But this time the moon was bright, and the backyard was illuminated in a bluish glow. I was worried about scaring the owls away. But I knew: if I wanted to see them, I would have to brave the cold, go outside, and let them see me. They could leave at any second, so there was no time to get dressed. I went to the back door, opened it quietly, and felt the cold spear me in the chest and scrape at my bare legs. I tiptoed out, barefoot in the piercing cold, in my gleaming white underwear. And I looked up at the roof.

At first I didn't see anything. But then one owl took flight. Then the other! They both flew right over my head—large silhouettes, their streaked chests barely visible in the bluish glow. And I watched as they flew northward into the moonlit sky.

Sadly, since that night, they have not returned.

It can be scary to show yourself. To *expose* yourself. And sometimes, when you truly show yourself to someone, they will leave. And that can be hard. You might start to think that you shouldn't have put yourself out there. You should've held back. If you hadn't shown yourself so completely, maybe they wouldn't have left.

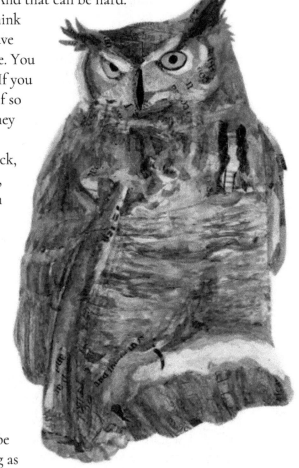

But if you hold back, you'll be stuck inside, just listening through a window.

Sometimes, to experience real beauty, you have to walk out into the piercing cold in your underwear. Sometimes real beauty— or even *salvation*— can be found only in exposing yourself. In allowing yourself to be *seen*. And in watching as they turn and fly away.

The Cedar Waxwing

Bombycilla cedrorum

When a father gives to his son, both laugh;
when a son gives to his father, both cry.

– Yiddish proverb

I have this hazy memory of my dad sitting in an armchair with his feet propped up on an ottoman, both legs in casts. Two long, white, plaster casts running the length of each leg—from hip to ankle. He's smiling and has a bushy '70s moustache. I'm not sure if this is a real memory that I have, or if it's just a photograph I've seen and I'm remembering the photograph.

My dad has this rare bone condition that makes his bones incredibly dense. I mean, so dense that he cannot swim—he sinks like a stone. And it's rare in the sense that only a dozen families have it, in the whole world. His bones are something like 2–3 times harder to break than regular bones. And he's probably 15–20 pounds heavier than other men of similar size. All this makes him sound a little like a superhero—which, of course, he is. But the downside is that this condition is incredibly hard on his body. The extra density and weight is hard on his joints—hard on his spine and hips. And as he gets older, the effects accumulate.

Sometime in the 1970s, when I was just a little kid and my dad was only around 30 years old, he had to get pins in his knees. That's why he had casts on both of his legs. And because he had pins in his knees—and heavy bones—my dad couldn't really play sports with his boys, as we got older. Overall, this was probably okay with my dad because he wasn't really much of a sports guy. But I did hear him say once that he regretted not being able to play sports with us, as we were growing up. I grew up the eldest of six kids—Jason, Jon, Jake, Joe, Jennie, and Jane. (Later, as I was moving out of the house and into adulthood, my parents adopted Jordan and Jarrod.) We played a lot of sports, as kids. And I think my dad wishes that he could've shared that with us a little more than he was able to.

One time, when I was in high school, my dad came outside to shoot hoops with the boys. We lived on 16 acres in rural Oregon, and near the house—next to a huge maple tree—our dad had poured a 20-by-20 concrete pad and planted an adjustable basketball hoop at one end. For his kids. And one afternoon, the four boys—me, Jon, Jake, and Joe—were out shooting hoops, and Dad came outside to shoot around with us. He couldn't shoot very well. And I'm pretty sure that it was the first—and only—time that I ever saw him try to run. But it was beautiful. We loved every minute of it. We laughed at how Dad couldn't shoot or run—and he laughed along with us, and kept trying. It was one of those childhood afternoons that stands out in my memory like a Rickey Henderson rookie card in a pack of commons.

Because my dad couldn't really play sports with us, we found other things to share. We watched a lot of movies together. And award shows. My dad *loves* award shows—anything where someone is being awarded something. The Oscars, the Grammys, Miss America—all the awards. I remember watching TV with my dad that night in 1983, when Michael Jackson did the moonwalk. I remember my dad's startled reaction: "Oh my goodness—did you see that?" We also did house projects together. We built decks, mended fences, remodeled bathrooms, installed ceiling fans, patched and repatched the basement wall that kept seeping. I mean, obviously my dad was the one who did all this—I mostly just handed him stuff when he needed it.

The point is: we did stuff together. It didn't matter *what* we did. Because the *who* always matters more than the *what*.

***

Did I mention that, growing up, the sport we loved most was baseball? My brothers and I *loved* baseball. We loved baseball so much (and our dad loved *us* so much) that, when I was in high school, our dad rented a small space on Main Street so that we could open a baseball card shop. We called it The Dugout, and it was a complete financial failure—not just because our small town wasn't big enough to support a baseball card shop, but also because my brothers and I had a habit of keeping all the best cards for ourselves.

Incidentally, did you know that there are three Major League Baseball teams named after birds? The Baltimore Orioles, the St. Louis Cardinals, and the Toronto Blue Jays. And the Baltimore Orioles have the distinction of sharing their entire name with a bird—the Baltimore Oriole. (The Baltimore Oriole is one of just four North American birds named after a city—the other three being the Cape May Warbler, the Nashville Warbler, and the Philadelphia Vireo.) A bunch of minor-league baseball teams also have bird names—including the Missoula Osprey, the Orem Owlz, the Sioux Falls Canaries, the Delmarva Shorebirds, the Great Lakes Loons, the Myrtle Beach Pelicans, the Akron Rubber Ducks (seriously), and my personal favorite: the Toledo Mud Hens. ("Mud hen"—or marsh hen—is a colloquial name for the American Coot).

They just changed the rules in Major League Baseball to try to speed up the games, and I have mixed feelings about that. Once, when I was a kid, I overheard some old guy comparing baseball to other sports like basketball and football, and saying the best thing about baseball was the absence of a clock. "There's no limit on how much time you have, to do what you gotta do," he said. "You catch the ball. You throw the ball. You hit the ball. You don't gotta think about anything else—and you don't haftuh worry about *time*. The game just lasts however long it lasts." And this was true. Nine innings could take two hours, or four. And the game could go more than nine innings.

The longest game ever played in professional baseball was played in 1981 between the Pawtucket Red Sox and the Rochester Red Wings. The game went 33 innings, lasting eight hours and 25 minutes.

What a glorious way to spend eight hours and 25 minutes!

This is how I feel when I go on my walks. There is no clock. A walk lasts however long it lasts. All I gotta think about is spotting the next bird. Or identifying the bird I just spotted. Of course, as a middle-aged man who has experienced—and continues to experience—a lot of hard things, I also gotta loosen up. I have to somehow uncoil the tension that has accumulated in my gut, and chest, and shoulders. But thankfully, the uncoiling happens naturally, as I step away from the clock and start walking—just thinking about spotting the next bird. Thankfully, I cannot obsess about all the hard things while trying to discern the chest markings on a sparrow through shaky binoculars—any more than I could obsess about all the hard things while chasing down a flyball in left field, or while leaning into an 80-mile-per-hour sinker.

Like baseball, the best thing about birding is that it has no clock. It elicits the same relaxed focus that is both laser-like and leisurely. The sort of focus that keeps you rooted in the present moment, where the only time is *now* and the game will last however long it will last.

My dad was 25 when my mom had me. And I was 25 when my wife had our eldest son, Cameron. I've always liked that symmetry.

As a young father, I really wanted my eldest son to like baseball. I wanted baseball to be one of the things that we shared, as father and son. I dreamed of playing catch together. Going to the ballpark together. Talking stats together—BA, HR, RBI, OBP. When Cam was eight years old or so, I coached his baseball team—his first year playing coach-pitch baseball. He was a decent contact hitter, and he had a good arm. But he didn't love it. He didn't really take to sports, in general. That year was the last year that he played baseball. And he played soccer for only a couple more years after that.

At 10 or so, he started teaching himself how to play the guitar—and from then on, music was more his thing. So—as he entered his teen years—instead of sharing baseball, we shared punk rock. He discovered Green Day and Blink-182. And I introduced him to The Clash, the Sex Pistols, and the Ramones.

I tell you all this so that I can tell you about the Cedar Waxwing. Waxwings resemble flycatchers (I'll tell you more about flycatchers later), but they aren't closely related to any other bird in North America. They have their own family (*Bombycillidae*) and their own genus (*Vieillot*). Altogether there are only three different species of waxwing—the Cedar Waxwing, the Bohemian Waxwing, and the Japanese Waxwing. And only the Cedar Waxwing is commonly found in the continental U.S. The Bohemian lives mostly in northern Canada and Alaska—though it can sometimes be seen in the northern half of the U.S. in the wintertime. (North Dakota is the Bohemian's idea of "flying south for the winter.") And the Japanese lives mostly in eastern Russia and northeast China, wintering southward in Japan and Korea.

In short: waxwings are nomadic northern birds. The Cedar Waxwing is the southernmost species. It summers in Canada and the northern states, and makes its way as far south as Texas—and even into Mexico—in the wintertime. Cedar Waxwings move in groups—sometimes in groups of just eight or ten, but often in groups so large that you can't possibly count them. I've seen huge candles of 50–60 waxwings, even 80–100 waxwings, arriving in November to flicker about the wicks of the tallest trees. They feed mostly on winter berries, but will also hawk bugs from the high branches. And they have a high-pitched, lisp-like call—*theeee theeee*—so high-pitched that it sounds like a hearing test. They're known for their yellow-tipped tails and the waxy red feathers on their wings—but these gorgeous little details are hard to see without a powerful zoom lens.

It is my impression that waxwings are popular birds. They seem to be a favorite among birders and nonbirders alike. And there's no denying that they are very beautiful. But to be honest, when I first started birding I didn't really care about the Cedar Waxwing. I'm not sure why. I just wasn't interested. When I would look through the lists of birds that I might find in Collin County, I never yearned to see the Cedar Waxwing. For whatever reason, it didn't *call* to me the way some other birds did.

On November 17, 2020, I had 57 species on my Life List but I still hadn't seen the Cedar Waxwing. And that morning, while I was out on my walk, Cameron called me from Utah to tell me that he needed help. He told me he had been struggling with severe depression for years. He was now 23 years old, and he told me he had been struggling since he was 14—maybe longer. As parents, we had never known. He had always seemed happy, responsible, healthy. He told me he had been hiding it—not wanting to upset or disappoint us. He told me why he was now calling me. He told me just how serious it had become.

I quit my walk and headed for the house. I booked a flight for the next morning—to go get my son and bring him home.

A couple days later, I took Cameron to Bonnie Wenk Park, hoping to show him a cool hawk or something, while we got some fresh air and spent some time together. We walked around the park and talked. He said he was feeling better—like a weight had been lifted off his chest. We didn't see any hawks. But as we crossed a small wooden bridge, we saw a flock of birds high in the treetops—so high that we could hardly make out what they were. With binoculars, we made out their crests and their black masks, and eventually we identified them as Cedar Waxwings. Then we finished our walk and drove home.

That was my first siting of the Cedar Waxwing. And waxwings are still not one of my favorite birds. But they have nevertheless become special to me. Not for their intrinsic beauty. Not for what they are. But instead, they are special because I saw them for the first time with my eldest son, who had called his dad and had come home because he needed help.

Cedar Waxwings are special to me the same way award shows are special to me. Because sometimes a thing is special not for what it is, but for who you share it with. Because the *who* matters more than the *what*.

The who *always* matters more than the what.

Winter

The Hooded Merganser

Lophodytes cucullatus

I'll let you be in my dreams,
if I can be in yours.

– Bob Dylan

Every hero's journey includes disaster. Facing disaster is part of what makes the hero a hero. Odysseus, Dorothy, Huck, Moana—they all faced disaster. Bilbo faced trolls, goblins, giant spiders, and a dragon. Luke faced a Death Star that could destroy entire planets. Katniss faced a bunch of murderous adolescents. The Prodigal Son? After losing all his money, he suffered through a famine and was reduced to feeding swine—and to wishing he could eat as well as the swine were eating.

In many myths and legends, disaster is associated with wintertime. In the Odyssey, the Men of Winter reside next to the Land of the Dead. And then there's that ominous line from *Game of Thrones*, foretelling disaster: "Winter is coming."

Usually, here in North Texas, winter isn't very ominous—or even very wintery. We've had a lot of balmy Christmases in the high 70s or even high 80s.

But in February 2021, during my first year of birding, we got hit by the Big Freeze, and it was a bona fide disaster. On February 10–11, 13–17, and 15–20, three separate winter storms swept across large portions of North America. And the storms hit particularly hard in Texas, where a massive power failure—the worst energy infrastructure failure in Texas state history—produced water, food, and heating shortages across the state.

In our neighborhood, which is divided by a bridge over Wilson Creek, one side of the bridge suffered rolling blackouts while the other side didn't. And we happened to live on the side that lost power. (Rumor had it that the other side was on the same grid as a nearby fire station, which explained why they were never deprived of power.) We were fortunate, insofar as our pipes never froze—so we were never without running water. But for about 10 days, our power rarely stayed on for longer than two hours at a time—so our house couldn't get warmer than about 50–55 degrees. Meanwhile, temperatures outside were hitting record lows. For a few days it was colder in Prosper, Texas, than it was in Anchorage, Alaska.

As I said, we were fortunate. As a family, the worst thing we faced was a chilly house and the repeated temporary loss of internet access, which kept cutting out for hours at a time. We counted our blessings, as we heard about others who had it much, much harder. More than 4.5 million homes and businesses lost power altogether. And at least 246 people died as a direct or indirect result of the crisis. Some estimated the death toll was as high as 702.

Obviously, nature itself can be one of the hard things that we face in life. And natural disasters are bigger than any of us. We can rarely survive them alone. It took thousands of volunteers to clean up after Hurricane Katrina, and again after Hurricane Harvey. During the Big Freeze, we took heart in hearing stories about neighbors helping neighbors. We donated what we could donate. And when our son needed reliable internet access to complete a school assignment, a neighbor from across the bridge invited us over.

Finally, when it seemed the worst had passed, my two youngest daughters and I bundled up to go for a walk through the neighborhood—just to get out of the house, after being homebound for nearly 10 days. It was still only 17 degrees. But the sun was shining and there were kids trying to push sleds across the iced-up pavement—a playful sign that the disaster had ended. On our walk, we discovered that the main pond was about two-thirds frozen over. But there, on the remaining open water and on the surrounding ledge of ice, were dozens of ducks and mergansers—roughly 60 waterfowl of seven different species, huddled on a small patch of not-yet-frozen water, weathering the storm together.

I mentioned earlier that I've always liked ducks. We owned pet ducks when I was in kindergarten. And the thing about ducks is that they can be ridiculously, fantastically ornate and beautiful. Have you ever seen the Northern Pintail? The Northern Shoveler? The American Wigeon? The Wood Duck? The Harlequin Duck? Those patterns and colors! Stop reading right now and look up some photos of these ducks, so you can see what I'm talking about. Even the common Mallard—just look at it, with its brilliant green head! And then there are the teals—the Cinnamon Teal, the Blue-winged Teal, the Green-winged Teal—each astoundingly gorgeous.

In case you were wondering: it seems there is no significant difference between ducks and teals. Apparently "teal" is just a name that has been given to certain smaller ducks. The order *Anseriformes* includes ducks, geese, swans, and other waterfowl. And within the order *Anseriformes*, the family *Anatidae* still includes ducks, geese, swans, and other waterfowl. And within the family *Anatidae*, there are multiple genera that include ducks of all kinds. The genus *Anas*, for example, includes the Northern Pintail, the Green-winged Teal, the Mottled Duck, and the Mallard. And the genus *Spatula* includes the Northern Shoveler, the Cinnamon Teal, the Blue-winged Teal, and the Garganey. What I'm saying is: ducks and teals are both spread across several genera, and there doesn't seem to be any great biological difference between a "duck" and a "teal."

Mergansers, on the other hand, are different. Unlike "teal," "merganser" is a name that actually denotes something. Mergansers are still in the duck family (*Anatidae*)—but they are a subset of waterfowl that have a long, narrow bill, distinguishable from the spoon-shaped bill more commonly associated with ducks. The genus *Mergus* includes the Common Merganser and the Red-breasted Merganser. And the Hooded Merganser has a genus all to itself (*Lophodytes*).

The Hooded Merganser is relatively small (about 16"), and the male has a blazing white crest and bright yellow eyes, while the female has a rusty-brown crest and darker yellow—sometimes orangish or even reddish—eyes. Both sexes are spectacularly beautiful.

I saw the Hooded Mergansers—a male-and-female pair—for the first time in December. They had their crests raised, as they paddled near a pair of Mallards. And they were so beautiful that I had to learn more about them. I learned, for example, that—like Wood Ducks—Hooded Mergansers will typically nest in a tree trunk, in an abandoned woodpecker cavity. In fact, Hooded Mergansers will sometimes nest *with* Wood Ducks—side by side, in the same cavity at the same time. And after I learned this, I started to notice something.

Throughout the winter months, I noticed that the waterfowl—the Mallards, the Buffleheads, the Lesser Scaups, the Ring-necked Ducks, the Gadwalls—they all seemed to get along just fine. They tended to congregate at this or that end of the lake, in this cove or in that cove. But they also seemed to stay in their groups—a congregation of waterfowl, comprising a group of Ring-necks, a group of Mallards, a group of Gadwalls, and so on. Like a neighborhood barbeque where the neighbors have all congregated but also—somehow, somewhat awkwardly—remain segregated.

But not so with the Hooded Mergansers. The mergansers seemed to mix and mingle. They might stay in pairs (male and female), but they mostly moved freely among the others. If there were 12 Mallards, they tended to stick together loosely as 12 Mallards; if there were 16 Ring-necks, they tended to stick together loosely as 16 Ring-necks. But if there were six mergansers, there were probably two among the Mallards, and two more among the Ring-necks, and two more over there, among the Gadwalls.

Later, in the spring—after most of the winter waterfowl had gone north—I kept seeing a lone male Northern Shoveler on the main pond at Whitley Place. Then one morning, as I was watching the shoveler, a female Hooded Merganser flew in. And instead of just landing anywhere on the pond, she flew straight over to the shoveler. And for several days, I watched this odd couple on the pond—the male shoveler and the female merganser—just hanging out, keeping each other company, until presumably they finally headed north.

Here, I must confess—though I probably don't have to tell you—that I can be a bit of an introvert. (I suspect most writers are somewhat introverted.) I sometimes find it hard to mix and mingle. The apt word is *taxing*. That is, the act of mingling takes something out of me. That doesn't make it a bad thing. I often enjoy socializing. But it still takes something out of me. (Going for a drive in the countryside can be lovely—but it still drains some gas from the tank.) And when interacting with others takes something out of you, often the easiest, most comfortable thing to do is to mingle only with the people you already know. But of course, this can be socially and spiritually limiting.

After watching the mergansers, I made a new goal for myself: at work-related "networking" events, and at church socials (and even just at church on Sunday mornings), I would try to have at least one brief exchange with at least three different people who I didn't already know—or who I hadn't talked to in a long time. Believe me: I wasn't very good at this. Most of the time I failed to achieve my goal. But when I did it—even when I talked to only one new person, for only 15 seconds—I felt better. More present. More *connected*.

Because we need other people. We need each other. We cannot survive all the hard things on our own. Ducks congregate because there is safety in numbers. And the Hooded Merganser taught me that we don't have to be the same to love and live with each other. You can mingle with a Mallard. You can nest with a Wood Duck.

Sure, at the neighborhood barbeque it can feel more comfortable to sit with the people you already know—or with the people who look more like you. But we're all just different ducks on the same pond. Once in a while, consider being the party's merganser. Consider moving among the Canvasbacks and the Buffleheads. Consider hanging out with the Lesser Scaups and the Northern Pintails. Maybe even look around for that one lone shoveler who has drifted away from the group and could use some company.

The Double-crested Cormorant & The Pied-billed Grebe

Phalacrocorax auritus
& Podilymbus podiceps

Life begins on the
other side of despair.

– Jean-Paul Sartre

Once I started venturing out of the neighborhood, Town Lake quickly became my favorite place to go walking. The park sits deep in one of Prosper's wealthier neighborhoods, east of Coit Street and south of Prosper Trail. Its main feature is the lake—a decent-sized reservoir that attracts weekend fishermen. If you pull up and look at the park from the little circle-shaped parking lot, it doesn't look like much. Some open grass, some trees by the lake. But if you get out and start walking east along the lake, you'll discover a four-wheeler trail at the top of a small ridge. And you can follow that trail around the backside of the lake, through thicker trees and open fields. It's a beautiful mixture of habitats, offering a wide variety of birds. And the unpaved trail takes you away from the neighborhood. The backside of the lake feels remote, secluded—the hidden coves undisturbed, undiscovered.

After I posted a few of my daily lists to eBird, Town Lake Park showed up on eBird's "Hot Spots" for Collin County. So I guess you could say that I discovered Town Lake Park for the birding world. And as of this writing, there have been 146 species reported at Town Lake—most of them reported by me. It's a great spot for sparrows, flycatchers, buntings, hawks, and—of course—waterfowl.

One of the birds that I discovered at Town Lake was the Pied-billed Grebe. Grebes are another family of waterfowl (*Podicipedidae*) different from ducks and mergansers. Whereas ducks can be divided into dabblers and divers, the grebes are all divers. And whereas ducks can be seen, from time to time, waddling along the shore, you will rarely—if ever—see a grebe on land. Grebes live almost entirely on the water. The Pied-billed Grebe's legs are set far to the rear of its body—in an ideal position for propelling the grebe underwater, chasing fish, but in an extremely awkward position for walking on land. Here in Collin County, we mostly see only the Pied-billed Grebe, and mostly only in the wintertime. But the U.S. also has the Horned Grebe, the Eared Grebe, the Western Grebe, the Least Grebe, and Clark's Grebe.

Another bird that I discovered at Town Lake was the Double-crested Cormorant. Cormorants are yet another family of waterfowl (*Phalacrocoracidae*) different from ducks and grebes. Cormorants are also divers—much bigger, deeper divers than the grebes. Here in Texas, we get the Double-crested Cormorant and the Neotropic Cormorant. On the West Coast, you'll also see the Pelagic Cormorant and Brandt's Cormorant. And on the East Coast, there's the Great Cormorant.

Throughout the wintertime at Town Lake, you'll see Pied-billed Grebes scattered among the ducks. And you'll often see a gulp of Double-crested Cormorants sunning themselves on the far dock, with their wings outspread.

Both the Pied-billed Grebe and the Double-crested Cormorant sit low in the water—sometimes with only their head and neck rising above the surface, like a submarine spyglass. On Town Lake, the grebe will be the smallest bird on the water and the cormorant will be the largest (unless a gaggle of geese happens to fly in that day). But aside from this difference in size, there's another interesting difference between these two birds.

Most waterfowl—including the grebes—secrete an oil (or "balm") that helps to waterproof their feathers. This is why water "rolls off a duck's back," as the saying goes. Water rolls off a grebe's back, too. And the advantage of having this balm is that the grebe's feathers stay dry—so the grebe can dive, resurface, and dive again, without having to dry its feathers. In contrast, the cormorants don't have this balm—or they don't have as much of it. This is why you'll see the cormorants out on the dock, sunning themselves with wings outspread. They have to dry their feathers between dives, or they'll drown. And this isn't a design flaw. The advantage of *not* having so much balm is that the cormorants are less buoyant and can therefore dive much deeper—enabling them to catch much bigger fish.

Okay, this might seem like a wild tangent, but we've reached the part where I have to say something about existentialism.

Albert Camus wrote about how "one must imagine Sisyphus happy." Sisyphus is the figure from Greek mythology who, having defied the gods, is condemned to push a boulder up a hill, over and over again. Each time he gets near the top, the boulder slips from his hands and rolls back to the bottom, and he must begin again, endlessly. According to Camus, life—ultimately—may be as meaningless as Sisyphus's repetitive task: we get up in the morning, we go to work, we come home, we go to sleep, then we begin again, endlessly. We repeat these tasks not because life has meaning, but only because we *choose* to keep going—even after recognizing the absurdity of it all. This is why "one must imagine Sisyphus happy": because otherwise, choosing to continue wouldn't make any sense. The implication is that, even if life is ultimately absurd and meaningless, we can still find happiness. And perhaps we can *only* be happy when we accept the ultimate meaninglessness of life—and nevertheless choose to continue.

Jean-Paul Sartre said something similar. (Which isn't surprising, seeing as Sartre and Camus were friends, and were both part of the Existentialist movement in the 1940s.) But Sartre didn't believe that life is absurd and meaningless. Instead, he—and his companion, Simone de Beauvoir—believed that life is full of meaning. But it is a meaning that we make for ourselves, from our choices, rather than a meaning that preexists us, or that exists outside of us.

What does it mean that we make meaning for ourselves? When we watch a baseball game, we are not watching a meaningless scenario in which people randomly swing sticks at a spherical object. We are watching *a baseball game*—an activity that has structure and meaning because we have, individually and collectively, chosen to give certain actions certain meaning. ("This is a pitch. This kind of pitch is a strike." *Etc.*)

For Sartre, making choices—doing something purposefully, because we have decided that it means something—is the ultimate exercise of freedom. There are moments when we realize just how radically free we are—when we realize that nothing constrains us but our own choices. And in these moments we experience *angst*. This is that unsettling sensation that we feel when we're driving near a cliff and we realize that—if we chose to—we could drive right over the edge. Nothing is stopping us. The weight of this freedom creates angst—a kind of despair. But once we recognize just how free we really are to make whatever meaning we want to make of our lives, that is when we are able to act purposefully. That is when life truly begins. Hence, for Sartre, "life begins on the other side of despair."

Thus, Camus and Sartre present two different ways of pressing forward. For Camus, we must accept the ultimate absurdity and meaningless of life. And for Sartre, we must recognize the radical freedom that we have to make our own meaning. Either way, the burden is on us: we must *choose* to press forward.

Now, I'm not saying that the grebe and the cormorant represent Camus and Sartre. It would be neat if the analogy mapped that way. But it doesn't. Instead, as I have struggled with the hard things—as I have struggled with my own various versions of despair—I have vacillated between, on the one hand, struggling with the ultimate meaninglessness of some things, and on the other hand, struggling with the weight of making some things meaningful. And always, always, I struggle with how to move through it—how to come out on the other side and keep pressing forward.

And as I have watched the grebes and the cormorants on Town Lake, I have realized that there are essentially two ways to survive the hard things and to keep pressing forward. Two different ways of coming out on the other side of despair.

Sometimes you become immersed in the hard thing, but you don't have to dive too deep. You're able to hold your space, to maintain some distance, so the difficulty doesn't penetrate your balmy feathers. You're able to swim through—and when you resurface, you're okay. Your feathers are dry. You could dive in again right away if you needed to.

But other times it doesn't work that way. Other times you become immersed in the hard thing, and you have to dive deep. The difficulty seeps into every crevice, soaking you to the bone. You manage to swim through—but when you resurface, you're waterlogged. If you dive in again, you'll drown. So you have to rest on the dock for a while. You have to stretch your wings and dry yourself in the sun before you can dive in again.

Neither way is the right way. The grebe is not superior to the cormorant, nor is the cormorant superior to the grebe. They're just two different types of divers—two different ways of being in the world. And maybe, in that sense, the grebe and the cormorant are like Camus and Sartre, after all.

What matters is pressing forward. We all, from time to time, become immersed in the hard things. If you need to be the grebe, be the grebe; and if you need to be the cormorant, be the cormorant. All that matters is that you resurface—that you do whatever you need to do to come out on the other side.

The Red-headed Woodpecker

Melanerpes erythrocephalus

> A dream unrealized...is the
> essential food of the soul.
>
> – Pam Houston

When I first started going for walks in Whitley Place, I would cut through the field behind the elementary school and make my way—through an opening in an old farm fence—down a slope to where the creek enters the northwest corner of the neighborhood. From there, I would walk along the creek, then I would cross the creek by walking across a sewage pipe. Then I would climb up the embankment to emerge on the paved path near the main pond—not far from the old snag where our Neighborhood Woodpecker lived.

This is a story about our Neighborhood Woodpecker.

Historically, many cultures have believed that woodpeckers can predict—and even summon—the rain. In Germany, the woodpecker is *Giessvogel*, or "pouring-rain bird." In Sweden, it's *ragnfagel*, or "rain bird." And in French they say the woodpecker calls *plue, plue, plue*, which is probably related to—or derived from—the word *pluie*, which means "rain." In Norse mythology, the woodpecker was associated with Thor, the god of thunder (which, of course, often accompanies rain). And the Pueblo likewise associated the woodpecker's drumming with thunder.

In Texas, we have a lot of woodpeckers. Rain? Not so much.

Actually, that's not exactly true. We don't get a lot of *days* with rain. But when it does rain, it *really* rains. When we moved to Austin in 2006, someone told me that Austin gets roughly the same amount of rainfall per year—in inches—as Portland, Oregon. The difference is that, in Portland, those inches accrue over 150 days of Northwest drizzle, whereas in Austin they accrue over 30 days of Southern downpour.

Anyway, the woodpecker family (*Picidae*) is one of my favorites. You've already heard about how Frankie became Bird #1 on my Life List. And Bird #12 on that list was the Downy Woodpecker—the second woodpecker I'd ever seen.

I saw my first Downy on the underarm of an oak tree, on my fifth birding walk through Whitley Place (after returning to Texas from that fateful trip to Oregon). At just 6", the Downy is the smallest woodpecker in North America—at the opposite end of the spectrum from the 19" Pileated Woodpecker. But despite its small size, the Downy seems to be the loudest drummer. Every time I hear loud woodpecker drumming and I search out the culprit, it ends up being a little Downy making all that big noise. I've heard other woodpeckers drum, and they aren't as loud.

Almost identical to the Downy is the Hairy Woodpecker. Both the Downy and the Hairy have black and white markings—and the male of each species has a little flare of red at the back of his head. At 8", the Hairy is bigger. But unless you see them side by side, it can be hard to tell these two woodpeckers apart. (I actually did see a Downy and a Hairy side by side one morning at Bonnie Wenk Park; they were about three feet apart, on a dead tree that protruded from the marshy area by the playground.) The best way to distinguish between the Downy and the Hairy is to focus on the size of the bill in relation to the bird's head. The Hairy's bill is thicker and longer—about the same length as the bird's head—whereas the Downy's bill is thinner and shorter than the bird's head. Here in Collin County, you can usually assume that the bird you're seeing is the Downy, because the Hairy is significantly less common.

Like the Downy and the Hairy (and most other woodpeckers) the Red-bellied Woodpecker has black and white markings. But both males and females have a red crown that extends down the back of their neck. The male's crown runs from forehead to nape, while the female's starts behind the forehead, which is grayish. By my count, Red-bellies are the most common woodpecker in this area. And they're very vocal. Even when I didn't see one, I often heard its *chur chur* as I walked among the trees.

Notably, the Red-bellied Woodpecker is named for a blush of red on its belly—but this blush is often faint and hard to see. It certainly isn't as vivid as the red crown on its head. The problem is: "black and white with red on its head" is a description that applies to lots of woodpeckers. So whoever had to name all the different species had to get creative. Once you've named the Red-headed Woodpecker, what do you call all the others? Personally, I think "Red-naped Woodpecker" would've been a better name for the Red-bellied Woodpecker—in part because the red nape is easier to see than the red belly, and in part because it would've mirrored the name of the Red-naped Sapsucker.

Sapsuckers are a subset of woodpeckers. They drill holes in trees like other woodpeckers, but they do it for the sap (and for the bugs that are attracted to the sap). We don't have Red-naped Sapsuckers in Texas—but we do get Yellow-bellied Sapsuckers in the wintertime. Yellow-bellies are one of the few woodpeckers that migrate. They come down to the Gulf States and Mexico from Canada. We had a Yellow-bellied Sapsucker that hung out in our neighborhood throughout the fall and winter, and I saw him on the same tree almost every time I passed by. Like most other woodpeckers, the Yellow-bellied Sapsucker is black and white with a red head—but it also has a distinct flush of yellow on its chest or belly. And I always identified it quickest by noting the stripe of white along the edge of its wing.

The one woodpecker that we get in this area that is *not* "black and white with red on its head" is the Northern Flicker. Flickers are fairly large woodpeckers (10–12"), and they have beautiful markings. They are brown with black streaks across their backs, a black jabot over a speckled breast, sometimes a dash of yellow in the wings and tail, a red "V" at the nape, and—for the male—a black handlebar mustache. Flickers are also interesting because, although they can hammer at a tree trunk like any other woodpecker, they prefer to forage for food on the ground, drumming the soft soil alongside the robins and sparrows. That struck me as odd the first time I saw it—like watching someone use a broadsword as a butter knife.

Supposedly Collin County also has the Pileated Woodpecker. But throughout my first year of birding, I never saw Frankie in Texas. Part of me wanted to track him down. But part of me also wanted to avoid him—to keep him special, as a bird attached to my childhood home in Oregon. Eventually, during my second year of birding, I saw Frankie several times in Denton County. But I still haven't seen him in Collin County.

Like the Pileated Woodpecker, the Red-headed Woodpecker is a striking bird. It's one of the few monomorphic woodpeckers—meaning the male and female both look the same. (In addition to being monomorphic, they are also monogamous.) They eat insects, spiders, centipedes, and millipedes, as well as seeds, nuts, and berries. But their bills aren't as good for drilling as other woodpeckers', so they typically nest in soft, rotting trees—often preferring a tall snag on the forest's edge. They live year-round in North Texas. But their population is declining, thanks to the decline in woodlands, so they are not frequently reported by birders in Collin County.

We had a Red-headed Woodpecker that lived near the creek in our neighborhood. The creek runs through a gully in the woods, near the main pond. And there was an old snag that stood at the edge of the woods, between the pond and the creek. I first saw our Neighborhood Woodpecker in mid-October, on that old snag—near a big hole that I assumed was its nest. And I saw our Neighborhood Woodpecker pretty regularly after that, for several months—almost always on or near the old snag by the pond.

Our daughter Ruby named our Neighborhood Woodpecker "Woody." When I first saw Woody, I didn't know what species Woody was because Woody's head wasn't red. It was dark gray. I learned later— after I figured out what species Woody was—that Woody's head would not turn red until spring. So I started getting excited. On my walks, I would search eagerly for the soon-to-be-Red-headed Woodpecker, hoping to track the blossoming brilliance of Woody's headdress over the coming months. Often, my walks through Whitley Place were focused *entirely* on finding Woody, hoping for a hint of redness.

The thrill of anticipation!

But in December they started paving the path that I had been walking through the field behind the elementary school. And in January they built a footbridge across the creek—about 50 feet from the sewage pipe that I had been walking across. And the construction drove our Neighborhood Woodpecker deeper into the woods. So most of my winter "sightings" of Woody were by ear, when I would hear Woody's distant rattling call. I caught only a few more glimpses of Woody on the old snag near the pond. Then a winter thunderstorm snapped the old snag in two. After that, I never saw Woody again.

Which means I never got to see any sign of Woody's red head-dress. Which was heartbreaking.

But Paul said, "Faith is the substance of things hoped for but not seen." And Emily said, "Hope is the thing with feathers." So I have hope and faith that Woody is still out there—somewhere—now with a fully blossomed, flaming-red head.

And I've realized that the dream of that unseen, blossoming red head produced its own pleasure. We all know the joy of anticipation from our childhood birthdays and holidays. But there can also be real joy in recognizing the potential that exists in others around us—even if we never get to see it fully bloom. This is the essence of faith and hope: recognizing *potential*. And faith and hope, even unrequited, can bring real joy.

The Orange-crowned Warbler

Oreothlypis celata

We must cultivate
our own garden.

– Voltaire

The Orange-crowned Warbler is the only bird in North America with the word "orange" in its name. There are other orange-colored birds—the Baltimore Oriole and the Blackburnian Warbler, for example. But, for whatever reason, the Namers didn't use the word "orange" when naming them.

And get this: an estimated 76 *million* Orange-crowned Warblers exist in the world. That's a lot, considering they live only in North and Central America. It's enough to be considered a fairly common warbler anyway. The most common warbler is probably the Yellow-rumped Warbler, affectionately known to some as the "butterbutt." And the least common warbler is probably Kirtland's Warbler, which can be reliably found only in Michigan.

Warblers are the darlings of the birder world, and it's easy to see why. They come in a wide variety of colors and patterns; they sing pretty tunes (hence the name "warbler"); and they're small and hard to spot, and typically can be seen only as they pass through town during spring or fall migration—so they present a rewarding challenge.

Depending on how you count them, there are 50–60 species of warbler in the United States. And over 40 warbler species have been seen here in Texas. But during my first year of birding, I saw only nine. (I told you: they present a challenge.) When I started birding in the fall—and then throughout the winter—I would often see a bouquet of butterbutts wafting from tree to tree. And later, during spring migration, I saw Yellow Warblers, Nashville Warblers, and one Blackburnian Warbler. (For an interesting anecdote about the Blackburnian Warbler, see the footnote on page 156.)

But throughout my first year of birding, I never once saw an Orange-crowned Warbler on any of my walks through Collin County. The Orange-crowned Warbler lives and breeds in Canada and the northern states during the summer—but it migrates to the southern states (and Central America) for the winter. That means there are three birding seasons—fall migration, winter, and spring migration—when the Orange-crowned Warbler is right here in my vicinity, just waiting to be seen. And there are 76 *million* of them. But somehow, throughout my first year of birding, I never saw a single Orange-crowned Warbler on any of my birding walks. Not one.

Stupid warbler.

Therapists and self-help gurus will tell you that, when there's a problem in your relationship with someone, you should resist blaming them and instead focus on what you need to change about your own behavior. For example, I've learned that I can be a bit of a chaser. When a problem arises, I chase it. I want to discuss it, to analyze it, to explain it, to argue about it, to apologize for it—all in my (sometimes misguided) effort to *resolve* it. I chase and I chase. And if the other person withdraws—if they run away—it only increases my urge to chase. Of course, wanting to resolve a problem is a good thing. And the other person's avoidance might itself be a problem. But— according to the therapists—instead of blaming the other person for their avoidance issues, I need to focus on my own chasing behavior, and on the underlying anxieties that drive it.

Stupid therapists.

***

The Orange-crowned Warbler is olive green, with a grayish head. As its name suggests, it has a patch of orange on its crown. But that patch of orange is tiny—and as the bird's Latin name implies, the orange patch is hidden. It isn't visible out in the field. So the Orange-crowned Warbler is pretty plain-looking, compared to most other warblers.

The Northern Parula, for example, has a plush blue-gray head and a bright yellow throat and breast, with a rufous spotted necklace. The Nashville Warbler has a blue-gray head, a bright yellow throat, breast, and belly, and a rufous cap. The Magnolia Warbler has a gray cap, a black mask, a bright yellow throat, breast, and belly, and a long necklace of thick black streaks. The Painted Redstart sports a black head and topside, with a fiery red belly and brilliant white wing patches. The Prothonotary Warbler is a sunny golden-yellow all over, with stark black eyes and blue-gray wings. And the Cerulean Warbler is a rich, streaky blue, with a snow-white throat and belly.

The Orange-crowned Warbler is downright drab, compared to these stunners.

Still, the Orange-crowned Warbler is a *warbler*. And it winters right here in our area. So as a new birder, I really wanted to see it. But after 49 birding walks throughout the fall and early winter, I still hadn't seen it.

As winter set in and it started getting colder, my walks started getting shorter, and I started spending more time at the window, watching the birds that came to the feeders I had hung in our backyard. The Mourning Dove, the Dark-eyed Junco, the Northern Cardinal, the Northern Mockingbird—these were our most common backyard visitors. But we also got the Yellow-rumped Warbler, the White-throated Sparrow, Harris's Sparrow, and sometimes a pair of Carolina Chickadees. Occasionally a Ruby-crowned Kinglet came through. And for a few days, we had a treasure of American Goldfinches.

***

At the start of December, I found a good log and brought it home to make a new birdfeeder. It's an easy DIY project: find a piece of tree, say 4–6" in diameter, and drill a bunch of different-sized holes all over it. Screw an eye hook into one end. Thread some twine or wire—or a bungy cord—through the eye hook. Hang the log from a tree so that it rests vertically against the trunk. Then stuff the drilled holes with suet (a lard-based bird food that you can find wherever they sell bird food). And voila! A log feeder.

I hung my log feeder on the oak tree in the back corner of our yard. And for several days, the suet was enjoyed mostly by the juncos and by the occasional Ruby-crowned Kinglet.

But then one afternoon a new bird appeared: a small, plain-looking, olive-green bird that nervously flew up to the log feeder, then away, then back again, then away, then back again. At first, I thought it was the kinglet. But there was something different about the way it moved. I grabbed my binoculars to get a better look from our bedroom window. And sure enough.

In my first year of birding, I went on 273 walks in Collin County, and I never saw a single Orange-crowned Warbler. But after I hung my homemade log feeder, an Orange-crowned Warbler graced our backyard on at least 34 days in December and January—including a stretch of seven days in a row.

I named her Mabel.

From Mabel, I learned that you don't always have to chase after the good things. Sometimes it's better to stay home. Tend to your own backyard. If you do that, then sometimes—instead of having to chase after the good things—the good things will come to you.

Spring

The Chipping Sparrow
Spizella passerina

> After winter must come spring;
> everything is everything.
>
> – Lauryn Hill

For the hero, after disaster comes recovery. And recovery always involves *change*. The Prodigal Son is humbled and repents. The cowering Bilbo morphs into a brave leader. Luke grows from farm boy to Jedi. The rapscallion Huck learns to see Jim as a human being, and finally does the right thing. Moana stops relying on unreliable Maui and steps up to save the island herself—by viewing the villain with empathy instead of fear. The hero's journey is always about transformation. The discovery of a new Self. The hero's recovery is a *rebirth*.

And rebirth, of course, is typically associated with spring. Spring means budding trees, blooming flowers—and birds migrating north for mating season.

Spring also means baseball. And before I tell you about budding trees and bird migration, I have to tell you a baseball story.

Phil Niekro was a knuckleball pitcher. Some pitchers are known for their fastball (like Nolan Ryan); some pitchers are known for their curveball (like Sandy Koufax); some pitchers had their own pitches, like Satchel Paige's "be ball"—so named because, in Satch's words, "it be where I want it to be." And Phil Niekro was known for his knuckleball.

In 1984, Niekro had won 284 games on his knuckleball. But going into the 1985 season, Niekro was 46 years old. Any other pitcher would have retired by that age. But Niekro was close to 300 wins—a huge career milestone. In 1984, only 16 pitchers had won 300 games, in all of baseball history. (As of 2022, only 24 pitchers have done it.) It's the sort of milestone that essentially guarantees a pitcher's place in the Hall of Fame.

Niekro had joined the New York Yankees in 1984. And in 1985, the Yankees were competing with the Toronto Blue Jays for the division title—which means they were winning a lot. On September 8, Niekro won his 299th game. And he was scheduled for five more starts, through the end of the season—which meant he would have five more chances to win #300. So things were looking pretty good.

But then Niekro and the Yankees lost on September 13. Then they lost again on September 18. Then again on September 24. Niekro pitched again on September 30—and this time the Yankees managed to pull off a come-from-behind victory that kept them in the pennant race. But because Niekro had given up the runs that had put the Yankees behind, he didn't get credit for their come-from-behind win. Niekro had had four chances to win #300, and he was still stuck at 299.

October 5 and 6 were the last two days of the season, and the Yankees and Blue Jays were playing each other in their final series. If the Yankees won on October 5, Niekro would be pitching in the last game of the season—with both the division title *and* win #300 on the line.

But the Blue Jays won on October 5, clinching the division title. This meant that the next day's game—the last game of the season—would be meaningless. So on the night of October 5, Niekro was trying to decide whether he should even bother pitching the next day. He could easily pull himself out of the lineup. And there were good reasons to do so. He'd already tried to win #300 four times and failed. It had been a long season. He was old and tired. His team was deflated after losing the title—and now, with the last game rendered meaningless, they might not play very hard. Not exactly the best conditions for winning his 300th game. Plus, Niekro would be a free agent after the season ended; the prospect of winning his 300th game next season could be used as a selling point—something another team could use to draw more fans to the ballpark. For all these reasons, it might be better to take a seat, to rest his old body over the offseason, and to go for #300 next year.

But then he got a wild idea. What if he tried to win his 300th game without throwing the knuckleball? The game was meaningless for the team, so why not have some fun with it? What did he have to lose?

So Phil Niekro—the greatest knuckleball pitcher of all time—took the mound on October 6, 1985, and got 26 outs without throwing a single knuckleball. (There are only 27 outs to be gotten in a nine-inning game.) And—miraculously—he also managed to get those 26 outs without giving up a single run. With two outs in the ninth inning, Niekro decided he couldn't get his 300th win without throwing the signature pitch that had earned him all his other wins. So he threw his knuckleball to strike out the final batter—and he became not only a 300-game winner but also the oldest pitcher in Major League history to throw a shutout.

The moral of the story, of course, is something like this: even if you've failed already, several times, just keep trying. Maybe shake things up a little—put a little twist on it. But give it one last shot. What have you got to lose?

This reminds me of another story. In The Book of Mormon, there's a prophet named Samuel. He belongs to a people called the Lamanites, so he's known as Samuel the Lamanite. And God tells Samuel to go preach to the people in a city called Zarahemla. But the people in Zarahemla cast Samuel out of the city. So Samuel is about to return home—he's about to give up—when God tells him again to go preach to Zarahemla. So Samuel goes back to Zarahemla. But the people won't let him into the city. It's enough to make him consider giving up again—but instead of giving up, he gets creative. Instead of leaving, he climbs onto the wall that surrounds the city and he starts preaching to the people from the top of the wall. He delivers a long sermon, calling the people of Zarahemla to repentance. And the people don't like this very much, so they start throwing rocks and shooting arrows at Samuel, who is still standing on top of the wall. But God protects Samuel so that he can't be hit by the rocks and arrows. And when the people see that Samuel cannot be hit by the rocks and arrows, they begin to believe that he's been sent by God, and they repent.

It's basically the same moral: even if you've failed already, several times, just keep trying. Maybe shake things up a little—put a little twist on it. What have you got to lose?

And this brings me to budding trees and bird migration. Some birds live in Collin County year-round, like the Northern Cardinal, the Eastern Phoebe, and the Red-tailed Hawk. Some birds winter here, like the Hooded Merganser, the White-throated Sparrow, and the Orange-crowned Warbler. Some birds summer here, like the Scissor-tailed Flycatcher, the Snowy Egret, and the White-eyed Vireo. And then there are birds that only pass through during migration—heading farther north in the spring or farther south in the fall. Spring and fall are exciting times because they mean migration—and migration means new birds passing through.

And of course, spring is *spring*. As Hopkins put it:

> Nothing is so beautiful as Spring—
> When weeds, in wheels, shoot long and lovely and lush;
> Thrush's eggs look little low heavens, and thrush
> Through the echoing timber does so rinse and wring
> The ear, it strikes like lightnings to hear him sing;
>
> ...
>
> What is all this juice and all this joy?

You get the point: spring is great. And as a new birder, with spring approaching, I was excited to see some new birds.

By March, I thought I had seen all the winter birds that I was going to see. I had seen the ducks—the mergansers, the pintails, the Buffleheads, the teals, the scaups, the Canvasbacks, the Gadwalls, the wigeons. I had seen the Yellow-rumped Warblers and Mabel, the Orange-crowned Warbler. I had seen a treasure of American Goldfinches. I had seen siskins and sparrows. So many sparrows!

Let me tell you about the sparrows. Lots of sparrows come to Texas for the winter. The most common—the one I saw the most, by far—was the White-throated Sparrow. I saw White-throats on almost every walk I took throughout the winter months. And I sometimes saw them by the dozens.

I also saw lots of White-crowned Sparrows, Song Sparrows, and Dark-eyed Juncos. Less common—but still plentiful—were the Field Sparrows, the Savannah Sparrows, Lincoln's Sparrow, and Harris's Sparrow. Harris's Sparrow, with its distinctive black face and pink bill, became my second-favorite sparrow—especially after one started visiting our backyard. And then there was the Fox Sparrow, the Clay-colored Sparrow, and the Spotted Towhee. I saw only a handful of Spotted Towhees and Fox Sparrows. And the Fox Sparrow immediately became my favorite, with its great name, its gray cheeks, and that gorgeous rust-colored blotchy pattern on its chest.

As winter was coming to an end, I had seen a dozen species of sparrow. But I hadn't seen the Chipping Sparrow. And although I *thought* I had once seen LeConte's Sparrow, I didn't feel very confident about it. So, as I was reviewing my Life List one day, I decided to delete LeConte's Sparrow.

That's the thing about sparrows: they can be hard to identify—hard to distinguish from one another. They tend to be ground-dwellers, staying low in the tall grass, in dense shrubs, or in the forest undergrowth. They belong to a large group of birds known among birders as "LBJs" (Little Brown Jobs)—birds that often require a closer look, and perhaps some study or experience, before they can be confidently (and successfully) identified.

As I said, at the end of winter I had seen a dozen species of sparrow, but I hadn't seen the Chipping Sparrow. I had heard they were common—and from time to time, I would see reports of sightings in the area. But I still hadn't seen them. I had tried again and again to go to the parks where Chipping Sparrows had been reported. But no luck. And as spring was beginning to bud, I was beginning to give up on seeing the Chipping Sparrow before it headed north for the summer.

One early spring Friday, I went to bed feeling discouraged. Disappointed. Depressed. Hard things were happening—again—and other things were not going the way I had hoped they would go. Normally, I would go to bed feeling excited about taking my walk the next morning. It was spring! There were new birds passing through! But on this particular Friday night, I considered pulling myself out of the lineup. And when morning came, I wanted to stay in bed. But I knew that staying in bed wouldn't help. So I got up and departed, hoping somehow my walk would work its magic. I knew it was still too early for migrating warblers—they wouldn't be here until April or May. Nevertheless, I hoped to see something new—or something special. Anything that might lift my sagging spirits.

I drove to Erwin Park and felt new pangs of frustration. It was a beautiful spring Saturday morning—so Erwin Park was packed with campers. The park sits a couple miles east of Prosper, and it is known for its mountain-biking trails, which run through the woods and across the open fields. If you follow the road into the park, you'll drive past a couple playground-and-picnic-table areas. And if you keep going, you'll see a small pond on your left, then you'll cross a small bridge over the creek and you'll hit a T in the road. At the T, it won't matter which way you turn because the road is a loop—so either way, you'll end up back where you are, near the small bridge. When I go to Erwin Park, I always walk the loop. You can leave the road here and there, to explore the trails through the woods and across the fields. You just have to watch out for mountain-bikers. Which is why it's better to go on a weekday.

That Saturday morning, I started walking the loop. But there were too many people around. Too many campers, too many bikers. Too many morning voices. Too many breakfast campfires. I tried to make the best of it. But the birds were scarce. I went off-road, and even off-trail a few times. But still I didn't see much. The morning air was clean and new. It was nice being outdoors, among the trees—much better than being in bed. But my discouragement from the night before still hung heavy. And the absence of birds left me feeling deflated. It was one of those rare occasions when my walk wasn't doing much to chip away the burden I was carrying.

I returned to my car, unlocked the door, and got inside. And I sat there for a few minutes, just breathing—trying to relax my shoulders, trying to slow-breathe my way through my discouragement. Then I decided that I couldn't go home yet. I had to do *something*. And for lack of any better idea, I decided to give it just one more try.

I was parked on the loop at a place called Hilltop Pavilion, near the park's restrooms. I got out of the car and walked to a small stand of trees that measures maybe 30 yards long and 10 yards wide. On my past walks, I had always circled clockwise around this small stand of trees, which had previously offered woodpeckers, waxwings, kinglets, thrashers—and the Fox Sparrow. But this time, on a lark, I decided to walk the other way around, counterclockwise.

And as I walked the other way around that stand of trees, I saw everything from a different angle. The same old trees became new trees. I stepped off the trail, yielding to an oncoming mountain-biker. And as I stepped back onto the trail, I caught a glimpse of movement, high in the budding branches of an oak tree. It took me a while to figure out what I was looking at—the birds were so small, and so high up. But eventually I made out their little rust-colored caps. The Chipping Sparrow is the smallest sparrow. And there, flitting from limb to limb, were three Chipping Sparrows.

I felt the weight lift, as I watched those little sparrows. And I had to wipe my eyes so that I could continue looking through my binoculars. No, I wasn't winning my 300th game. I wasn't dodging arrows to bring God's message to multitudes. I was just seeing a little brown bird for the first time. But on that particular morning, at that particular moment in my life, it felt like a victory. It felt like exactly what I needed.

And if there is one thing I have learned, it is that you cannot give up on what you need. You can't put it off or set it aside. Even if you've already failed several times—even if you've failed all winter long, or year after year. You have to give it another shot. Maybe shake things up a little—put a little twist on it. Just give it one more try. What have you got to lose?

It's true: "just one more try" won't always work. But sometimes it will. And if it is something you need, then it is worth just one more try. And even when one more try doesn't work, sometimes it still helps. Because sometimes what we really need is just to be able to say
that we gave it
one last try.

The Red-winged Blackbird

Agelaius phoeniceus

My job is not to look pretty
but to exist loudly.

– Mae Steed

Nora Haney Park is a small park, which is to say that it isn't much for walking. There's a small parking lot, a small playground area with a few small trees, a small field for throwing a frisbee around, and a small lake. And only about a third of the lake's bank is accessible from the park, because a neighborhood and a golf course border the other two thirds. In other words, there really isn't anywhere to take a *walk* at Nora Haney Park. The length of accessible lakeshore is not even 100 yards.

But for whatever reason, this small lake attracts a lot of waterfowl in the wintertime. So you can park and walk along those yards of accessible lakeshore and potentially see Lesser Scaups, Buffleheads, Canvasbacks, Ring-necked Ducks, Pied-billed Grebes, Double-crested Cormorants, Mallards, Northern Shovelers, Canada Geese, and maybe some Ring-billed Gulls. And you also might see a Belted Kingfisher, House Finches, Mourning Doves, Red-winged Blackbirds, a Downy Woodpecker, and George.

Obviously, you might not see *all* these birds every time you go—but I usually had pretty good luck when I visited. And Nora Haney is a good place to go when you really need to get out of the house but it's super cold outside—because you can look out over the lake from the parking lot, while sitting in your heated car.

One time, when I went to Nora Haney on a super cold day, another car was parked by the lake with an elderly couple sitting in it, looking out at the birds. We acknowledged each other. And eventually the woman rolled down her window and beckoned to me to do the same. Then she said, "What's that bird that keeps flying back and forth, making that *ack ack ack* sound, like a machine gun?"

She must have thought I would know the answer because I was using binoculars. "It's a Belted Kingfisher," I said.

"A Belted Kingfisher," she repeated, making sure she had it right. Then she waved her thanks and rolled up her window.

After that, I saw the same elderly couple at Nora Haney many times. When the weather was warmer, I stood next to their car and helped them identify other birds. (I never saw them get out of their car.) They really liked the Pied-billed Grebes. But they did not like the Red-winged Blackbirds.

"Oh no," said the woman. "They're too noisy." And she waved her hand in front of her face, as though referring to a bad smell. The man agreed and echoed: "Too noisy."

Red-winged Blackbirds nest in large groups, in the reeds or cattails that grow in marshes or alongside lakes or ponds. There's a racket of Red-winged Blackbirds that nests alongside the lake at Nora Haney Park. And they are definitely noisy.

When I think of blackbirds, I think of that Wallace Stevens poem, "Thirteen Ways of Looking at a Blackbird":

> I was of three minds,
> Like a tree
> In which there are three blackbirds.

In myth and folklore, and thus in literature, the blackbird often symbolizes magic or mystery. The blackbird is often the guardian of boundaries—of the line between life and death, between known and unknown—and thus it is associated with transition and transformation, with passing from one stage into another. And this makes me think of that Stevens poem again:

> When the blackbird flew out of sight,
> It marked the edge
> Of one of many circles.

After I started birding, I was surprised to learn that blackbirds are not closely related to crows. Crows belong to the family *Corvidae*, which includes crows, ravens, jays, and magpies. This means that the American Crow is more closely related to the Blue Jay than to any blackbird.

Blackbirds belong to the family *Icteridae*, which includes not only a variety of blackbirds but also a variety of cowbirds, grackles, orioles, and meadowlarks. Here in the U.S., we have the Bronzed Cowbird and the Brown-headed Cowbird, as well as the Common Grackle, the Great-tailed Grackle, and the Boat-tailed Grackle. In North Texas, cowbirds and grackles (along with European Starlings) are the birds that you see congregating in Walmart parking lots, in great Hitchcockian flocks of hundreds or even thousands, scavenging for food and releasing a cacophony of buzzes and cackles. Our own local Walmart has installed a speaker that plays buzzing bird sounds that—I assume—are meant to shoo away the noisy masses. It is safe to say that the cowbirds and the grackles are considered pests. And the cowbird is doubly despised for its habit of laying an egg in another bird's nest—where its chick will often outmuscle the other bird's chicks, in the struggle for food and attention. Some birds have faced the threat of extinction, thanks to the Brown-headed Cowbird's parasitic nesting practices.

On the flipside, the family *Icteridae* also gives us the Hooded Oriole, the Orchard Oriole, Scott's Oriole, Bullock's Oriole, and the Baltimore Oriole—as well as the Western Meadowlark, the Eastern Meadowlark, and the Chihuahuan Meadowlark. In contrast to the cowbirds and the grackles, which are despised, the orioles and the meadowlarks are beloved. Six states have named the Western Meadowlark as their state bird (Kansas, Montana, Nebraska, North Dakota, Oregon, and Wyoming). And the Baltimore Oriole is Maryland's state bird—and the namesake of Major League Baseball's Baltimore Orioles. The orioles and the meadowlarks are beloved and renowned for their bright yellow and orange coloring, and for their singing. The meadowlarks, Scott's Oriole, and the Baltimore Oriole all have especially beautiful songs—and the Orchard Oriole's song is perhaps my very favorite of all birdsongs.

It is fascinating that the family *Icteridae* can give us both the cowbirds and the orioles. Both the good and the bad—both the despised and the beloved. You might say that life is like the family *Icteridae*. Sometimes you get the oriole's song. And sometimes the cowbird lays an egg in your nest.

And then there are the blackbirds. Here in the U.S., we have the Rusty Blackbird, the Yellow-headed Blackbird, the Tricolored Blackbird, Brewer's Blackbird, and the Red-winged Blackbird. If the cowbirds and the grackles are despised, and the orioles and the meadowlarks are beloved, then the blackbirds are somewhere in the middle. Like the orioles and the meadowlarks, the blackbirds can be colorful and visually attractive. (Go look up some photos of the Yellow-headed Blackbird.) But like the cowbirds and the grackles, the blackbirds congregate in large flocks and make buzzy, rasping, screeching noises that are hard to describe as "singing."

It is as though the blackbirds exist on the edge—on that boundary between lovable and despicable—where they could go either way.

In 2013, when we moved to Prosper, our second child, Mae, was just entering high school. Like our eldest, Cameron, Mae had taken to music, becoming a passionate pianist by the age of 12. As a new kid at Prosper High School, Mae entered a singing contest that was open to kids and adults of all ages—and won. At 15, Mae was the only contestant who both sang and played their own accompaniment (on the piano, of course). And although I'm biased, you have to believe me when I tell you: Mae was amazing.

But transitions can be hard. Despite this victory, being a new kid at Prosper High School didn't go so well for our little Mae-mae, who was struggling with social anxiety and—we learned later—with much bigger questions about relationships and identity. Mae didn't share the same interests as the "popular" girls who would gather in large flocks and out-muscle Mae in the struggle for attention. Most of the time, Mae felt marginalized, outcast. On the edge. And alone.

At 18, as a senior, Mae wrote a poem that included lines like:

> My job is not to look pretty
> but to exist loudly.

And:

> To say 'I love myself' is
> the simplest revolution.

In June, shortly after the world shut down, Mae left home at 21 to get married. And in February, at 22, Mae returned home in tears.

Some nights, as Mae worked through the sadness by belting out ballads on the piano, I would stand in the hallway, on the other side of the wall, where the piano chords would vibrate the framed photo of our six-month-old Mae-mae. And I would weep quietly, as Mae sang a song about the courage it takes to find one's place in the world.

In the spring, our family went out for fancy burgers at a place where we could sit outside on the patio, socially distanced. Grackles were edging close, hoping for scraps, when we heard a chattering cry from a nearby tree.

"Is that what they sound like?" Mae said, referring to the grackles that had gathered near our table.

"No, that's a Red-winged Blackbird," I said, nodding at the bird in the tree.

"It isn't black or red," Mae said.

"That's a female," I said. "The males are black with red on their shoulders."

"It's *loud*," Ruby said.

"I like it," Mae said.

A few days later I took Mae to Nora Haney Park, to show her the Red-winged Blackbirds. That morning, the blackbirds were out and loud. Their call is a shrill trill—almost a shriek. And when 40 or 50 Red-winged Blackbirds are shrieking over the reeds, in the early morning, it's quite a sound. Some might say it's like fingernails on a chalkboard. Robert Penn Warren refers to it in a poem:

> If singing is what you call that rusty, gut-grabbing cry
> That calls on life to be lived gladly, gladly.

Mae watched the blackbirds move from reed to reed, and across the lake and back. We walked around a bit, and saw some other birds—Mallards and grebes out on the water, a gang of Blue Jays in the trees. And we talked a bit, too. Mae talked about trying so hard for so many years to be liked and accepted, to be the person that others expected them to be. And about how this never worked. And then Mae told me about how they weren't going to do that anymore. About how they needed to be true to who they were. And we returned to the blackbirds, still moving about in the reeds at the edge of the lake, and still screaming.

"They're loud, aren't they," I said.

"I love them," Mae said, putting their hands together under their chin. They seemed happy. It felt—as we stood there, listening to the racket of blackbirds—like we were passing together from one stage into another.

As we drove away, Mae asked me if I had a favorite bird. I told them that this was a hard question. It was like trying to name a favorite child—I could probably name five. But finally I admitted that I was partial to the Blue-headed Vireo.

"What about you?" I said. "Do you have a favorite?"

"The Red-winged Blackbird," Mae said, confidently. And they seemed pleased—as though they had found something they had lost a long time ago.

"That's a good one," I said.

And we rode the rest of the way home in silence.

Don't be afraid to be who you are. To love what you love. Sing your song—even if it's a shriek. Forget about being despised or beloved by others. One person's cacophony is another person's symphony. Embrace transitions. Exist loudly.

This is what I've learned from Mae, the lover of blackbirds.

The Osprey

Pandion haliaetus

> I am not a writer. I have been
> fooling myself and other people.
>
> – John Steinbeck

Only one of our five children would go for walks with me regularly. I got Cam (Child #1) and Mae (Child #2) to go out with me only once or twice, each. Jackson (Child #3) was always a flat-out "Nope, not interested." (He's the least outdoorsy of all of us.) And while Sophie (Child #4) would *talk* a lot about going out with me, she went out with me just once, right after the Big Freeze. Only Ruby (Child #5) was ever excited about going for walks with Dad. *She* would often ask *me* if we could go for a walk together. When I saw Bird #100, the Snowy Egret, Ruby was with me. In fact, it was Ruby who spotted the egret flying overhead, and pointed it out to me. (Later, after I deleted a few birds from my list, the Snowy Egret dropped to #96—but it was still an exciting moment when it happened.)

I tell you this because I'm going to tell you a story about one of the times when I was out on a walk with Ruby. But you won't understand the significance of what we saw unless I tell you some other stuff first.

The author Neil Gaiman tells a story about how, one time, he went to a party for Accomplished People, where he chatted briefly with "a very nice, polite, elderly gentleman." The two chatted about several things—including the fact that they shared the same first name. And then at some point the other Neil said: "I just look at all these people, and I think, what the heck am *I* doing here? They've all made amazing things. I just went where I was sent." And Gaiman replied: "Yes. But you were the first man on the moon. I think that counts for something."

I love this story for lots of reasons. One of the hard things that many of us face is imposter syndrome—that feeling that we don't belong where we are because we're not as deserving as others. The worry that soon everyone will discover the fraud we have perpetrated on them. I know I have this problem. Have I mentioned that I'm a lawyer? That's my day job. And there have been many times when I've been standing in a room full of high-powered people, and I've looked around and thought: "What the heck am *I* doing here?"

And I've discovered that my own imposter syndrome can run in two different directions. Sometimes it's about underselling myself—thinking I'm not half as good as everyone else, at the thing we're all trying to be good at. And other times it's about overselling others—thinking they're 10 times as good at the thing we're all trying to be good at. And if all these people are 10 times better at this thing than I am, then obviously they're all much more valuable *as persons* than I am. So what the heck am *I* doing here?

This tendency to overestimate the admirability of others reminds me of Rogers Hornsby. (Yes, I'm going to talk a little more about baseball.) Growing up, I loved playing second base. And anyone's list of All-Time Greatest Second Basemen will likely include Rogers Hornsby. Growing up, my favorite *active* second baseman was Ryne Sandberg—the Chicago Cubs' future hall-of-famer. But Rogers Hornsby was on another level—a legendary second baseman of mythic proportions. As a kid, I included Ryne Sandberg with Hornsby, Joe Morgan, Nap Lajoie, and Jackie Robinson on my top-five All-Time Greatest list. I would put Sandberg at #5 because he was still young. Then I would waffle on how to order Morgan, Lajoie, and Robinson, #2 through #4—the order could change daily. But Hornsby was always #1, no question. His stats were incredible. He hit over .400 three times, hit .402 over a five-year span (1921–1925), and hit .358 over the span of his 23-year career. That lifetime batting average is the third highest in Major League history. And he's the only player to ever hit .400 with 40 home runs in the same season (1922). Who wouldn't put Hornsby at #1?

But as an adult, I include Hornsby on my top-five list only grudgingly—with an asterisk by his name—because I really don't want to include him at all. As an adult, I've learned that Hornsby was notoriously nasty. His teammates unanimously hated him. He was frequently traded away to other teams because he was so toxic in the clubhouse. His second wife said that he "laid violent hands on her" numerous times. His third wife committed suicide one night, after having dinner with him. He had a serious gambling problem. It has long been believed that he was a member of the KKK—though this has never been confirmed. And whether he was a card-carrying member or not, he was certainly a confirmed bigot, antisemite, and racist. Who wants a guy like that on their "All-Time Greatest" list?

In short: Rogers Hornsby is the perfect reminder that we should be careful about overestimating the admirability of others. As a kid, I dreamed of being like Rogers Hornsby. But now I would much rather be a smalltown second-string second baseman who plays nice with others, than be Rogers Hornsby.

And this brings me to the Bald Eagle. Here in America, we all grow up with iconography that portrays the Bald Eagle as strong, proud, bold, majestic—a fierce and dominant predator of mythic proportions, at the top of the food chain. The perfect symbol of our Great Nation.

But the Bald Eagle is like the Rogers Hornsby of raptors. That is, the Bald Eagle isn't actually the majestic, admirable, dominant predator that our iconography makes it out to be. Turns out, the Bald Eagle is a thief. Comparatively speaking, it isn't a very successful fisher or hunter, so it tends to steal food—mostly fish, but sometimes rodents or other prey—from other predators, after they've done all the work of catching it. Indeed, the Bald Eagle's reputation as a thief and plunderer was so well-known at the time, that Ben Franklin objected to making it our national mascot because he thought it would send the wrong message. (Franklin thought the Wild Turkey would be a more noble, more respectable choice.)

And have you ever heard the Bald Eagle's cry? No, it isn't the fierce shriek that you hear in the movies. Moviemakers almost always dub-in the fierce shriek of the Red-tailed Hawk when they show a Bald Eagle, because in real life the Bald Eagle's cry is a weak, wheezy-sounding squeak—like a worn-out dog toy.

If the Founders wanted a fierce, majestic predator for our national bird, they should've chosen the Osprey. The Osprey is slightly smaller than the Bald Eagle but it is—in my opinion—much more beautiful. And Ospreys are far better fishers. They can hover momentarily over the water before diving. And according to some estimates, they succeed in 25% of their dives. So mythic is the Osprey's fishing prowess that some Native American tribes believed that their own fishing would be enhanced if they rubbed their hooks with the oil from an Osprey's body. You'll often see Ospreys and Bald Eagles together, over large lakes and reservoirs—where Ospreys are frequently the victims of the Bald Eagle's thievery.

Unfortunately, Ospreys don't live in North Texas. They spend their summers in the northern states and Canada, and their winters on the Gulf Coast, so they only pass through this area during migration. The same is basically true for Bald Eagles—though Bald Eagles can sometimes be seen here in Collin County throughout the winter.

In Collin County, our most common raptors are the Red-tailed Hawk, the Red-shouldered Hawk, and Cooper's Hawk. The Red-tailed Hawk is probably the most common hawk nationwide (and year-round). And Cooper's Hawk is also pretty common—both nationwide and year-round. Here in Collin County, I would say the Red-shouldered Hawk is slightly more common than Cooper's Hawk. But the Red-shouldered Hawk exists only in the eastern half of the United States, and along the West Coast. You won't see it in the Great Plains or the Intermountain West. (I'll tell you more about the Red-shouldered Hawk later.)

In the winter, or during migration (both spring and fall), we also see the Sharp-shinned Hawk and Swainson's Hawk. The Sharp-shinned Hawk is basically a smaller version of Cooper's Hawk—and the two can be hard to tell apart sometimes. And in the summertime, Swainson's Hawk basically lives where the Red-shouldered Hawk doesn't: throughout the Great Plains and the Intermountain West. It passes through Texas on its way to Argentina for the winter.

The accipiter family also includes kites and vultures. As far as I can tell, "kite" is just another word for hawk—though the kites tend to be smaller than most of the hawks. The only kite that we see regularly in North Texas is the Mississippi Kite, which summers throughout the South. But down near the Gulf, you can see White-tailed Kites and—if you're lucky—maybe a Swallow-tailed Kite. And of course, vultures are common nationwide. One thing I didn't know until I started birding, however, is that there are actually two species of vulture in the United States. Growing up in Oregon, I knew only about the Turkey Vulture, which is the most common vulture and the only one that exists nationwide. But in the southern and eastern states, you can also see the Black Vulture. The Black Vulture's sense of smell isn't as strong as the Turkey Vulture's—so Black Vultures will often follow Turkey Vultures around, relying on them to sniff out rotting carrion for dinner.

***

All these raptors are graceful fliers, with wings made for soaring on air currents. And every time I see a raptor riding high on the wind, I think of that Hopkins poem:

> I caught this morning morning's minion, king-
>> dom of daylight's dauphin, dapple-dawn drawn Falcon, in his riding
>> Of the rolling level underneath him steady air, and striding
> High there, how he rung upon the rein of a wimpling wing
> In his ecstasy! then off, off forth on swing,
>> As a skate's heel sweeps smooth on a bow-bend: the hurl and gliding
>> Rebuffed the big wind. My heart in hiding
> Stirred for a bird—the achieve of, the mastery of the thing!

Talk about mythologizing. This is basically how my mind views the accomplishments of others around me: "The achieve of, the mastery of the thing!"

My favorite of all the raptors might be the Osprey. While hawks, eagles, and kites all belong to the same family (*Accipitridae*), the Osprey is different, belonging to a family of one (*Pandionidae*). As far as I can tell, the main difference between the Osprey and the hawk family is in their feet. Osprey have rounded talons instead of grooved talons. And their outer toe is reversible—a trait they have in common with owls. This allows them to carry their prey with two talons in front and two talons behind, instead of three-and-one. The Osprey's unique feet features (feet-ures?) are part of what make it uniquely proficient at catching fish—which is probably why the Bald Eagle sometimes finds it easier to take a fish from an Osprey than from the water.

If you haven't watched an Osprey soar and hover and swoop and dive—and come up with a fish in its talons—then you seriously need to reorder your priorities and get yourself to the nearest lake. Go to the Pacific Northwest during summertime or to the Gulf Coast during wintertime, or to Florida during anytime. Ask around for the nearest Osprey. Then prepare to exclaim: "The achieve of, the mastery of the thing!"

***

One early spring weekend, I was feeling pretty low, with a serious case of imposter syndrome. I had missed something at work—or, rather, a competitor had seen something that I had failed to see—and this had enabled him to gain an advantage over me in a case that we were arguing. And I couldn't help but think: "The achieve of, the mastery of the thing!" I felt like my competitor was certainly much better at this job than I was. All my colleagues and competitors were giants in my field—mythic in their proportions. What business did *I* have being in the same room with them?

That Sunday afternoon, Ruby asked if I wanted to go for a walk. (She could probably sense that I was feeling down and needed to get outside.) I said, "Sure," and I suggested that we go out in the kayak on Town Lake. Ruby liked going out in the kayak. She was 10 at the time, and in the kayak she would sit up front, keeping a handwritten list of the birds we saw on a small yellow notepad. We once saw a beaver dragging a long stick through the water, and Ruby named the beaver Bea. We followed Bea until she dove underwater and didn't come up again. And next to her list of birds on the small yellow notepad, Ruby wrote "Bea," with one tally next to the name.

That Sunday afternoon, out on Town Lake, Ruby and I saw George. We saw swallows and a kingfisher. We saw bluebirds, cardinals, and chickadees; cormorants, grebes, and Mallards; sparrows and a Brown Thrasher. But I couldn't shake my doldrums. I still felt depressed about having to face mythic-sized giants at work, as someone so small.

Then a large, white-breasted raptor flew from the trees, out over our heads. I tried to twist around in the kayak, to get a better look, but it flew past the horizon of trees. I speculated that it might've been an Osprey—it seemed much bigger than a hawk. But Red-tailed Hawks can have white breasts, too, and are common around Town Lake. And I didn't get a very good look, so I couldn't be sure.

At the end of our voyage, Ruby and I climbed out of the kayak and onto the dock. And as we turned toward the shore—there it was! The Osprey, hovering just over the trees, at the edge of the lake, near the dock. It was so big! So magnificent! As Ruby and I watched it hover for a moment, I whispered: "Isn't it amazing?" And in my head I thought: "The achieve of, the mastery of the thing!"

And then it pooped. Like, a *lot* of poop. The sheer amount of poop was startling. It was like someone pouring a pitcher-full of milk from a three-story window.

"Holy smokes," I said. And Ruby burst out laughing. The reverent moment of awe had been shattered. Shat upon.

And I was reminded of that children's book, *Everyone Poops*. Your boss poops, your parents poop. All-star athletes poop. Celebrities, too. The most magnificent people you can think of—they all poop. Even the majestic Osprey takes a dump now and then. We all make a mess sometimes. Even the best of us.

Yes, I had missed something at work—but there had been plenty of other times when I had caught something that someone else had missed. And that same competitor who had just shown his brilliance had completely blown it in a previous case. Because he's human too. Like the rest of us.

Don't mythologize the people around you. And don't sell yourself short. If you're in that room with those other folks, then you probably deserve to be in that room with those other folks. Repeat that to yourself:

I deserve to be here.

The Common Yellowthroat
Geothlypus trichas

I come into balance.
I begin again.

– Ofelia Zepeda

When I was a kid, we used to drive from Oregon to Utah in the summertime to visit Grandma Steed. Grandma Steed lived in a buff-colored brick house. The front lawn was kept short—the grass prickly under our bare feet. And the back patio was covered in bright green astroturf. Grandma kept a porcelain cookie jar on the kitchen counter, full of vanilla-cream cookies, and a crystal candy dish in the living room, full of multicolored hard ribbon candy.

One hot afternoon, when we were playing in the backyard, I turned and ran across the astroturf patio, heading into the house, and ran—*BAM*—forehead-first into the sliding-glass door. I didn't see that it was closed—didn't see it coming. And the glass door shattered all around me. I remember trying to jump right up, but then feeling wobbly and sitting back down. And I just sat there, on the astroturf patio—stunned, dazed—not entirely sure what had just happened. It took me a while to put the pieces together, before I could stand up and continue.

Much later, as a 22-year-old college student, I met a guy named James in my philosophy class. It was January. The semester had just started, and we each caught the other scanning the classroom for a familiar face. We became fast friends—mostly as rock-climbing partners. And that summer, my roommates and I moved into a basement apartment next door to the big house that James shared with six or eight housemates. (The number was always changing.)

I was at James's house one morning, just as the fall semester was starting, when there was a knock at the door. I answered it. And there, standing on the porch, was a fantastically beautiful young woman in a peach-colored, floral-patterned dress. She had a sprinkling of freckles across her collarbone, and long ringlet curls the color of wheatfields. She smiled brightly and introduced herself as Michele—James's sister. And the first thought that formed in my brain was, "I could definitely be James's brother-in-law."

Michele and I ran into each other a few more times after that. Then we spent a couple hours together, while Michele did her laundry at James's house. Then we started spending *all* our hours together. And by Thanksgiving—maybe earlier—I knew things were serious.

James would ask me now and then how things were going between me and his sister. And the following March, it was James who delivered roses to the table at the restaurant where Michele and I were eating dinner, on the night that I proposed.

After we were married, Michele and I moved into a different basement apartment, on the other side of campus. And James would come over to watch TV and eat our cereal. And after we had Cameron, our first child, James would try to show him how to play the guitar—and would get confused every time he rediscovered that a six-month-old isn't quite ready to learn guitar.

When he had girlfriends, James would ask us what it was like to be married, what it was like to have kids—and what we thought about his girlfriend. And whether he had a girlfriend or not, he would confide in us that he wasn't sure about ever getting married, or about ever having kids. Not long after college, he quit his high-paying sales job and traveled around the world for a year. And after that, he lived mostly off the grid— surfing, climbing, making music, making art, working odd jobs—and smiling peacefully at anyone who tried to tell him that he wasn't living his life the way it was supposed to be lived.

When Michele and I had two young kids, and we were on vacation with Michele's side of the family, James and I stayed up late one night, just the two of us, talking about life and God and literature—and about the philosophies that we had studied together in that philosophy class.

On January 8, 2014—roughly 20 years to the day after I met James in that philosophy class—Michele's dad called to tell us that James had been shot and killed by a police officer. He had been going door to door, hoping to make a little money by shoveling snow from people's driveways, and a neighbor had reported a "suspicious" man in the neighborhood. The officer who arrived was overly aggressive in his questioning, which put James on the defensive. And instead of deescalating the situation, the officer got more aggressive, eventually reaching to grab James. Things got physical. James was killed. And now, young officers watch a training video that shows bodycam footage of what happened to James, as an illustrative example of how *not* to handle a situation.

The news about James hit us like a wall—a wall we didn't see coming. We were cruising along, living life, when—*BAM*—life shattered all around us. We were dazed. We struggled to put the pieces together. And it took a long while before we could stand and continue.

Back in the old days, birding was done with guns. Men—including the famous John James Audubon—would go out and shoot a bunch of birds and then retrieve the carcasses to figure out what they'd shot.

Eventually, women started using opera glasses to watch birds out their window. And as spyglass technology improved—and as women's influence in the ornithology community grew—scientists and birding associations started trading their guns for binoculars. And we shifted from identifying dead birds to identifying living ones.

***

The first time I saw a Common Yellowthroat, I thought it was dead. The Common Yellowthroat is a warbler with a song that goes *witchity-witchity-witchity-witchity*. Yellowthroats live in South Texas year-round, and come up to North Texas (and farther north) only in the summertime. Like most warblers, they're very small (4–5"). But unlike most warblers, which tend to populate the tippy tops of tall trees, Yellowthroats prefer the tall grasses and reeds of meadows and marshes.

The first time I saw a Common Yellowthroat, it wasn't in a meadow or marsh. Instead, it was on our back patio. I saw it as I was taking out the garbage. The bird was lying on the patio, knocked out cold. We have three large windows in our living room that look out over the patio and into the backyard, and they reflect the trees along the back fence. So, from a birds' perspective, our three large windows look like three large portals into an extended part of the backyard—three large gateways to more trees. Sadly, we've had a lot of birds run into our windows. It's a real problem that we still haven't solved.

A while back, a female cardinal died after running into our window. And over the winter, we had a Yellow-rumped Warbler and an American Robin that both knocked themselves out. In the spring, in addition to the Yellowthroat, there was a Chimney Swift and a Ruby-throated Hummingbird. And once, while the whole family was watching TV in the living room, we were startled by the loud *thunk* of a Cooper's Hawk hitting the window. (It recovered immediately, without hitting the ground, and turned to glide away from our wide-eyed stares.) I'm sure there have been more—these are just the ones that I know of.

When I see (or hear) it happen, I run to see if the bird is okay. If it's on the ground, I go outside to scoop it up in my hands, to try to resuscitate it—to protect it, while it regains its bearings. I brought the Yellow-rumped Warbler inside, out of the cold, and it got loose in the house for a while. So when the robin hit, I just held it outside in the freezing cold. The robin came to almost immediately after I picked him up. But he just sat there in my hands, dazed, trying to put the pieces together. I stood there holding the robin in my hands for almost 20 minutes, before he was able to fly off.

One time, a House Sparrow knocked itself out on the window, and when it came to in my hands, it panicked and tried to fly off too soon. It flew erratically, lopsidedly, and ran into the brick side of our house. I picked it up again, trying to help, and it flew off again—too soon—and ran into the fence. I picked it up a third time, but as I picked it up, it had some kind of seizure and died in my hands. I've always wondered if it would have lived if it had just rested—if it had just taken a moment to collect itself—before trying to continue.

When I saw the Yellowthroat, I picked it up in my hands—its tiny chest palpitating with rapid breaths. It was a female (less colorful, no black mask), and I cradled her in my hands as I sat on the patio chair and waited. After a few minutes, she rolled to her feet, still wobbly. She allowed herself to be held as she inspected her surroundings—my hands, the patio, *me*. And after a few more minutes—after getting her bearings—she fluttered off to the safety of the bushes by the back fence.

Sometimes the hard things hit us like a wall. We don't see them coming, then—*BAM*. A cancer diagnosis at a routine checkup. An offhand remark that slices us open. A phone call on a Thursday morning. And suddenly everything is in pieces.

When this happens it's okay to sit for a while. You might feel wobbly. Don't try to fly too soon. Find the hands that will scoop you up. Allow yourself to be held while you get your bearings. Take all the time you need, before you continue.

The Green Heron

Butorides virescens

It's okay if you're lost;
we're all a little lost.

– Jane Marczewski

Back in October, when I returned to Texas from Oregon (after meeting Frankie), I was excited to go find George again. But I didn't see George on my first walk through the neighborhood. Instead, at the main pond, I saw a Great Egret—the slightly smaller, all-white version of George.

At nearly five feet tall, with a six-foot wingspan, George (the Great Blue Heron) is the largest heron in the United States. And at over three feet tall, with a four-foot wingspan, the Great Egret is the second-largest heron in the United States. Egrets are part of the heron family (*Ardeidae*), and—as far as I can tell—"egret" just means "all-white heron." There's the Great Egret, which is large and all white, with a yellow bill; there's the Snowy Egret, which is medium-sized and all white, with a black bill and yellow feet; and there's the Cattle Egret, which is medium-sized and all white, with a yellow bill and a slight blush of orange on its head and chest in the summertime. The only exception to this all-white trend among egrets is the Reddish Egret, which does have a "light morph" that is all white but also has a "dark morph" that looks similar to the Little Blue Heron.

Despite its name, the Little Blue Heron is not just a smaller version of the Great Blue Heron. The Great Blue Heron is a light powdery blue with a pale gray neck and a blue-and-white head. But the Little Blue Heron is a much deeper navy blue with a deep red—call it burgundy—neck and head. As I said, the dark morph of the Reddish Egret resembles the Little Blue Heron—but its neck and head are lighter, more like a rusty brick red, instead of burgundy.

Then there are the night-herons, which supposedly hunt mostly at night, though you can still see them during the day. My favorite is the Yellow-crowned Night-heron, with its bold black-and-white face. And there is also the Black-crowned Night-heron, with its comparatively stubby neck. There's a heronry of Black-crowned Night-herons at a lake near downtown Dallas, where I have seen as many as 14 Black-crowned Night-herons at once.

The American Bittern and the Least Bittern are also part of the heron family. They're both mostly brown, with streaky brown-and-white necks that blend in with the reeds. The Least Bittern—at just a foot tall—is the smallest heron in North America, and very difficult to spot (in my limited experience).

I love the herons. All of them. The heron family is one of my favorites. I love how herons appear to be solitary birds—typically hunting solo at the water's edge—but back at the heronry, they nest in large groups of 12, 40, even 80 birds. Sure, they look like loners when you see them at the lake. But they've got plenty of family back home.

I mentioned earlier that I was bullied as a kid, after skipping a grade. But the bullying wasn't limited to being called "the Brain." I was smallish for a sixth grader. And after skipping a grade, I was less than five feet tall as an eighth grader. The eighth-grade hallways and locker rooms were hazardous for a kid my size. And at the start of ninth grade—as we were sitting in health class, learning about how babies develop, with a colorful transparency on the overhead projector showing us what a bisected pregnant woman looks like—I said something to the other boys sitting near me, trying to join them in their snarky banter, and one of them let loose with a string of snark aimed directly at me, capping it off with "you fetus."

The classroom erupted in laughter. There were chants of "Fee-*TUSS*, Fee-*TUSS*." Then there were follow-up jokes about how they should handle me delicately because my bones hadn't ossified, and because I still had a soft spot on my head. You know: the usual fun that freshman boys make.

But the nickname stuck. From that day forward, I was known as "The Fetus" when being referred to in third person— or just "Fetus" when being addressed directly. ("Is the Fetus coming? Oh, hey Fetus, how long have you been standing there?") And it wasn't just the boys. The girls called me Fetus, too. It was my nickname until I graduated.

Of course, I'm much taller now. And I've grown enough to be able to laugh about silly high-school nicknames. But that day in ninth grade, after we got out of health class, I went and sat in a bathroom stall and cried for a while. And over the next two years—until I finally hit my growth spurt—I spent a lot of time climbing out of dumpsters and nursing bloody noses. Apparently, there was something about a tiny kid called the Fetus that agitated the older, bigger boys. Something that made them want to pick me up and throw me into various containers.

One time, at scout camp—after I'd been pantsed in front of the group and thoroughly ridiculed—I wandered away, into the woods. I followed a trail for a while, then I left the trail and weaved through the trees until I found a massive fir that had fallen across a dry creek bed, like a bridge. I climbed onto it and walked back and forth across that bridge, asking God for some kind of sign that he existed. Because I really wanted God to exist, but I just wasn't feeling it.

I walked back and forth across that fallen bridge until the afternoon heat broke and the evening coolness started drifting in. I felt alone—but not lonely. As a 14-year-old, I hadn't yet immersed myself in poetry. But now, as an adult recalling that 14-year-old experience, I'm reminded of that famous line by Marianne Moore: "The cure for loneliness is solitude."

I felt peaceful and safe there in the trees—there *with* the trees. Those furrow-barked firs, straight as telephone poles, with ferns scattered at their feet. And after a while, it occurred to me that maybe this feeling of peace and safety was the sign I had been asking for. That maybe God *was* there with me, in the trees. (I would learn later, as a grad student, that the word *tree* derives from the same Indo-European root as *truth*.)

Eventually, I found my way back to camp, where everyone was sitting down to a campfire dinner. I took my seat on a stump near the fire. And when one of the adult leaders asked me where I had been, I shrugged and said, "In the woods." He tilted his head and raised one eyebrow. And I couldn't tell if his look was meant to scold me for wandering off, or if he was just mentally marking me as a weirdo.

The first time I saw the Green Heron, I saw three of them. Green Herons live year-round on the Gulf Coast, and they'll wander up to North Texas in the warmer months. They're much smaller than George but they eat the same things: frogs, snakes, crawdads, fish. And they're known for dropping bugs on the water for bait, snatching the small fish that rise to take the bug. In my experience, Green Herons can sometimes be hard to spot, not just because of their smaller size, but also because they tend to stay in or near the reeds, instead of out on the open bank.

I was at Nora Haney Park in April, after most of the waterfowl had left to migrate northward. Only a few Pied-billed Grebes, a handful of Canada Geese, and some Lesser Scaups remained on the lake. So my attention was focused on the springtime swallows swooping over the water and out over the field by the playground. To get a better look at a Northern Rough-winged Swallow that kept looping back and forth over the lake, I stepped down closer to the bank—and that's when I flushed three Green Herons from the cattails. The first let out a *kuk kuk kuk* as it flew across the lake, disappearing into the cattails on the other side. Then two more flew up into the elm tree next to the playground.

I watched the two herons in the elm tree for a long time—partly because these birds were new to me, and their iridescent-green feathers were so beautiful. And partly because it struck me as so incredibly weird to see these two long-legged herons twenty feet up, perched among the leaves of an elm tree—as though they thought they were warblers. It was the sort of thing that I wanted other people to see—that I wanted other people to know about—because of the oddity of it. I thought surely I was seeing something that no one had ever seen before. Herons in a tree! It felt like big news. Hot gossip.

But the herons didn't do anything exciting. They just sat there, safe in the high branches of the elm tree—waiting for me to leave. I wandered off, chasing after the swallows. And when I came back later, they were gone.

That afternoon, on the internet, I discovered that what I had witnessed wasn't weird at all: Green Herons, like most herons, *nest* high in trees. They go high in the trees all the time. Yes, they hunt low in the reeds by the water. But trees are their *home*. And I felt this revelation settle into my shoulders, and down into my belly, like a sign.

There's a Robert Frost poem where one character says, "It all depends on what you mean by home." And then the other character responds: "Home is the place where, when you have to go there, / They have to take you in."

When the hard things happen, go wherever you need to go to feel safe. Take some time in a bathroom stall. Take a walk in the woods. Sure, some people might raise eyebrows, or say things. They might mark you as a weirdo. But that's only because they don't understand who you are. You do whatever you need to do—you go wherever you need to go—to feel safe. Fly home if you need to—wherever home might be. And stay there for however long you need to stay.

Home is there for you. That is what home is for.

The White-winged Dove &
the Red-shouldered Hawk

Zenaida asiatica &
Buteo lineatus

When the power of love overcomes the love of power,
the world will know peace.

– Jimi Hendrix

The dove has symbolized something resembling peace since the Torah and the *Epic of Gilgamesh*. Both of those ancient books have stories about a flood. And during that flood, both Noah and Gilgamesh send a dove to look for dry land. The dove returning with an olive branch signaled the end of hard things—and something resembling the arrival of peace.

Later, in 1798—as American democracy was just getting off the ground following the Revolutionary War—there was talk of entering another war, this time with France. American politics had already splintered into two parties: the Federalists (including John Adams and Alexander Hamilton) and the Democratic-Republicans (including Thomas Jefferson and James Madison). And when the Federalists started pushing for another war, Jefferson wrote a letter to Madison describing the Federalists as "war hawks."

Still later, in 1949—not long after World War II had ended—a collection of individuals and organizations convened in Paris for a meeting they officially called the World Congress of Partisans for Peace. Less formally, it was known as the Paris

Peace Congress. Earlier that year, Pablo Picasso had produced a striking lithograph of a white dove against a dark background, called *La Colombe* ("The Dove"). And this lithograph was used on the poster for the Paris Peace Congress. That Paris meeting led to the formation of a permanent organization called the World Peace Council, or WPC. And the WPC adopted Picasso's *La Colombe* as its logo—making the dove an official symbol of postwar peace and pacifism.

But it wasn't until the 1960s that "hawk" and "dove" became common stand-ins for "militant" and "pacifist." The first pairing of these political proxies appeared in a 1962 article in *The Saturday Evening Post* about the Cuban Missile Crisis. The article described those who favored using an air strike to destroy the Cuban missile bases as "hawks," and referred to those who favored a blockade as "doves." This comparison between hawks and doves became more popular during the Vietnam War, as LBJ was repeatedly labeled a hawk and anti-war protesters painted flower-filled doves on their protest placards. And in 1968, DC Comics launched a comic-book series called *Hawk and Dove*. In 1969, the famous Hawk 'n' Dove bar opened on Capitol Hill. That same year, posters started appearing, advertising the Woodstock Music & Art Fair. The festival was billed as "3 Days of Peace & Music." And the posters used a now-famous drawing by Arnold Skolnick of a white dove perched on the neck of a guitar.

I've already told you about most of the hawks that we see here in Collin County. (We're back to talking about birds now—not politicians.)

As for the doves, Collin County has four: the Mourning Dove, the White-winged Dove, the Eurasian Collared-Dove, and the Inca Dove. The Mourning Dove is the most common dove throughout North America. And the Eurasian Collared-Dove has also become common throughout most of the U.S.— though it doesn't exist in the Northeast. In contrast, the White-winged Dove, though common where it exists, exists only here in Texas, and in the southern halves of Arizona and New Mexico. (It exists throughout most of Mexico, too—which is geographically part of North America when talking continents, but more commonly associated with Central America when talking regions.) Finally, the Inca Dove occupies the same southern range as the White-winged Dove—but it is relatively rare here in Collin County. I never saw the Inca Dove during my first year of birding. But I saw lots of the other three doves.

Elsewhere, Hawaii has the Zebra Dove, Florida the Common Ground Dove, and the West Coast (including Oregon) the Band-tailed Pigeon. And of course, *everywhere* has the Rock Pigeon—that urban bird beloved by Bert that most of us know as simply "the pigeon."

The Rock Pigeon is also commonly known as the Rock Dove. (Pigeons and doves belong to the same family, *Columbidae*, with doves being generally smaller and slenderer than pigeons.) The Rock Pigeon, originally native to Europe and North Africa, was named the "Rock Pigeon" because, in the wild, it resided in rock formations, nesting in cliffs and crevices. But it was domesticated. Then it was brought to the New World in the 1600s. The United States' Rock Pigeon population is descended from domesticated pigeons that escaped or were set free—and they live and thrive almost entirely in human-populated areas. It's uncommon to see a Rock Pigeon far from pavement.

Now let me tell you a Buddhist story about a hawk and a dove. King Sibi was a ruler in ancient India. A devoted Buddhist, Sibi had pledged to prevent all beings from suffering. So Indra (the Hindu king of deities) and Viśvakarman (one of his underlings) decided to test Sibi by transforming themselves into a hawk and a dove. The hawk then chased the dove, trying to eat it, and the dove sought refuge with Sibi. The dove begged Sibi not to let him be eaten—and the hawk conversely begged Sibi not to let him starve. So, to save both birds, Sibi offered his own flesh to feed the hawk. The hawk agreed, but asked that Sibi give him an amount of flesh equal to the weight of the dove. Sibi placed the dove on a scale and allowed a butcher to carve his flesh and weigh it against the dove. But no matter how much flesh the butcher carved from Sibi's side, the dove—which was really the deity Viśvakarman—still weighed more. Finally, Sibi climbed on the scale to show that he was willing to offer his whole self to feed the hawk and to save the dove. Moved by King Sibi's virtuous intentions, Indra and Viśvakarman revealed themselves, and Indra restored Sibi's flesh.

I like this story because it is about giving one's whole self for the protection of others—both prey *and* predator. And I like it because it is also about the willingness to sacrifice one's whole self in devotion to moral principles.

I also like it because it highlights an important reality: that harm cannot ever be fully prevented. The hawk will eat the dove—*must* eat the dove. And not only is this harm unpreventable; we shouldn't even want to prevent it. Because sometimes certain kinds of harm are a necessary part of life. Sometimes doing what appears to be harmful is also doing what is good—what is necessary to survive. And sometimes the effort to avoid harm (like King Sibi's effort to prevent the hawk from eating the dove) will only produce greater harm (like the loss of King Sibi's whole self for the sake of a deceptive dove).

This reminds me of Abraham Lincoln. Lincoln believed fervently in the moral rightness of preserving the Union—and he believed that the Civil War was necessary to preserve the Union. To avoid doing harm, he could have allowed the South to secede. He could have allowed the Union to dissolve into two separate nations, one with slavery and the other without. But he believed dissolution would constitute an even greater harm. So—like the hawk eating the dove to avoid starvation—he fought the Civil War to avoid dissolution.

For a while, we had a pitying of White-winged Doves coming to our backyard. And one spring afternoon—when my wife Michele was sitting on the couch, and I was standing at the window—I saw a pair of White-winged Doves on the small round table that sits in front of our thuja trees. The male kept fanning his tail and doing a funny little dance across the table, while the female watched.

"I think Loverboy is trying to get himself a date," I said.

Michele followed my gaze out the window and said, "Oh, how sweet. How come I never get a funny little dance?"

So I turned from the window, and I did a funny little dance, sliding in my socks across the living room floor. And Michele laughed brightly, her laugh like coins falling into a purse.

A week or so later, at Bonnie Wenk Park, I watched a pair of Red-shouldered Hawks chasing each other through the treetops—screeching at each other. At first, I thought the hawks were fighting over territory. I had frequently seen one Red-shouldered Hawk at Bonnie Wenk Park—but I had never seen two. And the screeching was fierce. Piercing. The chase vigorous and aggressive. Then one of the hawks tried to land on top of the other. And I realized it was another mating ritual.

In *H Is for Hawk*, Helen Macdonald talks about raising and breeding goshawks. (I don't recall whether Macdonald identifies the specific species she is referring to, but here in North America, the Northern Goshawk is one of the largest hawks we have—nearly as large as an Osprey.) Macdonald talks about how breeding hawks is not for the faint-hearted—about how there's "a very fine line between goshawk sexual excitement and terrible, mortal violence." According to Macdonald, you can't just put a pair of goshawks in an aviary and leave them to it. Because—more often than not—"the female will kill her mate."

When I got home after watching the Red-shouldered Hawks and their screech-mating, I told my wife about it—about how I thought, at first, that they were going to kill each other, but then it turned out that they actually loved each other.

And Michele said, "That sounds about right."

Because humans can be a bit like hawks sometimes. That is, sometimes there's a fine line between sexual excitement and violence. The starkest and darkest form of this line manifests itself in horrible acts of sex trafficking and rape. But we see the line emerge more subtly in everyday relationships, too—even in *good* relationships. The people we're most capable of hurting are those we love, and those who love us. (Cue the old Mills Brothers' song, "You Always Hurt the Ones You Love.") Jealousy, manipulation, betrayal, resentment—these are all just milder forms of violence, often descended from romance or sexual excitement.

In May 2021, after nearly 26 years of marriage, my wife and I were considering divorce. Some of the hard things had gotten so hard that we had started to think maybe we could resolve some of those hard things by doing a different hard thing.

But then a miracle happened. We realized we were screeching at each other because—like the Red-shouldered Hawks—we *wanted* to be together. (Someone once said that the true death of a relationship is not anger but indifference.) With this realization, we stopped seeing each other as enemies fighting over territory, and we went back to seeing each other as vigorous partners chasing each other through the treetops.

And as I pondered the mating rituals of the hawk and the dove—the funny little dance, and the vicious screeching—it became clear to me that love is not a feeling. Love is not the heady waft of romance or the visceral pull of sexual excitement. Love is a decision. A sustained series of decisions. Our decisions may be *motivated* by certain feelings. And our decisions may *produce* certain feelings—which might, in turn, motivate more decisions. But it is a mistake to confuse love for a feeling. Love exists in the decisions we make—in whether we choose loyalty over betrayal, trust over suspicion, vulnerability over defensiveness, forgiveness over blame. We say we "fall in love" or we "fall out of love," like it's an accident outside our control. But these metaphors are wrong—and perniciously self-serving. We talk like this to avoid accountability. We say things like, "We can't choose who we love." But this is self-delusion. Of course we can choose. It is never an accident. We *choose* to linger longer by the door, hoping to catch a glimpse of that person. We *choose* to send that text, or to accept that invitation to lunch. We *choose* to see that person in the best possible light—or in the worst. We *choose* to love that person. Or we choose not to.

And choosing love means choosing harm. There will be disappointment, frustration. Heartache. Pain. We're not hawks—but we're human. None of us can avoid hurting those we love, or being hurt by those who love us. Love is risk. You can't choose trust without risking a breach of that trust. And we can make some of our most loving decisions only *after* we have been harmed. Our most intentional, most meaningful decisions to trust come *after* trust has been broken. And the most loving decision we can ever make is to forgive—an act of love that we cannot perform until *after* we have suffered harm.

Of course, sometimes the harms are too great. Sometimes choosing to love that person really is too risky, and the healthier choice is to walk away. "Should I stay or should I go" is always a question of which harm is greater. It is the same as Lincoln's dilemma: Do you fight the war to preserve the Union, or do you dissolve the Union to preserve the peace?

I don't know the answer. But I do know that both the Red-shouldered Hawk and the White-winged Dove mate for life. And I know that, if it feels like you're in a war, the key is to remember what the screeching is for. The hawks screech because they *want* to be together. And the doves? Well, I also know that, once in a while, it helps to do a funny little dance across the living room floor.

Summer

The Dark-eyed Junco
Junco hyemalis

It depends on where you sit,
how you stand.

– Rufus E. Miles

After departing, after facing disaster, and after recovering from that disaster, the hero returns home. Moana returns to her island. Bilbo returns to the Shire. Katniss returns to District 12. Dorothy returns to Kansas. ("There's no place like home.") And the Prodigal Son returns to his father's arms. Sometimes the location or nature of "home" might be different. (Luke's new home is with Leia and the Rebels, after his home on Tatooine is destroyed.) But the hero always returns home, changed for the better. That's the whole point of the hero's journey: you go out into the world, you face the hard things, you recover, and then you return a better person *because of* the journey.

Now, this will sound like another detour, but let me tell you about Rufus E. Miles. Miles worked for the administrations of four different U.S. presidents—Truman, Eisenhower, Kennedy, and Johnson. He was working for Truman in the Bureau of the Budget, just after World War II, when one of his examiners was offered a position at another agency for a higher salary. The examiner had overseen the budget of the other agency, and had been quite critical of that other agency—and now he was torn: Should he remain loyal to the Bureau or leave for a higher salary at an agency he had criticized? He told Miles about his dilemma and asked if the Bureau could match the new salary. But Miles said that wasn't possible. So—for the sake of his family— the examiner went to the other agency for more money.

After the examiner left, Miles told one of his associates: "Just watch! Within three or four months he'll be critical of the Bureau and defensive of his new agency." The associate disagreed, praising the examiner's objectivity. But Miles insisted it was only a question of how long it would take.

About six months later, Miles's prediction came true. And Miles turned to his associate and said: "You see: it depends on where you sit, how you stand." The associate was impressed and said, "That deserves to be given the status of a law." And Miles's Law—rephrased as "where you stand depends on where you sit"—became a new axiom in Washington.

Miles's Law, of course, is just a clever way of restating an ancient truth (and a law of physics) that every artist knows: that your perspective is tied to your location, and that changing your location will change your perspective.

By the way, I find it interesting that we use the word "locate" as a synonym for "find"—as in, "I'm trying to locate my phone." But we use the word "relocate" as a synonym for "move," instead of as a synonym for "re-find." If you think about it, "relocate" *could* mean "re-find." For example: if a pizza place is located on Main Street—meaning it can be found on Main Street—and then the pizza place relocates to Maple Street, we could say that the pizza place can now be re-found on Maple Street. And I like the idea that, when we relocate (or move) something, we also re-find it.

In July, our family took a trip to see more family—first in Monmouth, Oregon, then in Spokane, Washington. With the COVID pandemic still raging, traveling had been *verboten*. So the only trip I had taken, since the world had shut down in March 2020, had been that fateful trip to see my parents—the trip that had included my encounter with Frankie. But now that more than a year had passed since the shutdown, and we had all been vaccinated, we decided things seemed safe enough for a summer trip to see family. And I started getting excited about the prospect of seeing new birds in the Northwest.

In Spokane, my wife's brother and his family live on five acres just north of the city—not far from what immediately became one of my favorite birding trails, Indian Painted Rocks (on the Little Spokane River). There, I saw Red-breasted and Pygmy Nuthatches, Mountain Chickadees, Black-billed Magpies, Red-naped Sapsuckers, Canyon Wrens, and Bullock's Oriole—13 new species, total.

And in Oregon, I saw Black-headed Grosbeaks, Bushtits, Black-throated Gray Warblers, Purple Finches, Violet-green Swallows, Chestnut-backed Chickadees, Bald Eagles, Marsh Wrens, Brewer's Blackbird, and Steller's Jay—28 new species, total. After five days in Oregon and five days in Spokane, my Life List jumped from 124 species to 165. It was exhilarating.

Of course, now that I've been birding in Oregon multiple times during different seasons, I've learned that Polk County (the area where I grew up) offers a list of staple birds that is different from—but analogous to—the list of staple birds in North Texas. Here in Collin County, you can go for a walk just about any time of year and you're almost sure to see Northern Cardinals, Northern Mockingbirds, Blue Jays, House Finches, the Carolina Wren, and the Carolina Chickadee. And in Polk County, Oregon, you can go for a walk just about any time of year and you're almost sure to see American Robins, Spotted Towhees, California Scrub-Jays, Purple Finches, the Pacific Wren, and the Black-capped Chickadee. And in both counties, you'll regularly see Red-tailed Hawks, Great Blue Herons, and Mourning Doves. The two parallel lists of staple birds look something like this:

Collin County, TX	Polk County, OR
Northern Cardinal	American Robin
Northern Mockingbird	Spotted Towhee
Blue Jay	California Scrub-Jay

House Finch	Purple Finch
Carolina Wren	Pacific Wren
Carolina Chickadee	Black-capped Chickadee
Red-tailed Hawk	Red-tailed Hawk
Great Blue Heron	Great Blue Heron
Mourning Dove	Mourning Dove

The first two birds on each list are, by my count, the two most frequently seen birds in each region. And the rest of the birds on each list are the most frequently seen birds from their respective families—jays, finches, wrens, etc. But it's worth noting that Collin County has only one species of jay and only one species of chickadee, whereas Polk County has two of each—and both are common. That is, in Oregon I've seen almost as many Steller's Jays as California Scrub-Jays, and almost as many Chestnut-backed Chickadees as Black-capped Chickadees. So Polk County's staple list could easily include both species of jay and both species of chickadee. Similarly, White-winged Doves don't exist in Oregon, but in Collin County I've seen almost as many White-winged Doves as Mourning Doves. And I've also seen almost as many Red-shouldered Hawks as Red-tailed Hawks. So Collin County's staple list could easily include both species of dove and both species of hawk.

Anyway, the point is: every place has a different view. If you want to change what you see, change where you are.

When we started planning our July trip to Oregon, our then-13-year-old daughter Sophie and I decided that we would go on a quest to find the Dark-eyed Juncos that had left us. The Dark-eyed Junco is a species of sparrow—a winter bird in Texas—readily identified by its black or dark-gray head, white breast, and pinkish bill. William Stafford has a poem about juncos, in which he refers to their "clean little coveralls."

Like other sparrows, juncos are mostly ground feeders. They are known for "double scratching" (hop-scratching with both feet, simultaneously) when they look for seeds and insects. And they usually travel in groups. Throughout the winter, we had a mulch of six or more juncos in our backyard almost daily. They would hang out under the feeders, eating the seeds that fell to the ground. And I saw juncos on nearly every winter walk that I took—at nearly every location that I visited. It almost got boring to see them. They were everywhere.

Eventually, I learned that Sophie had started calling the juncos "Karen." One day, a junco lit on the back patio, and she said, "There's Karen."

I said, "You named it Karen?"

Sophie nodded.

I said, "How can you tell that *that* one is Karen?"

And she shrugged and said, "They're all Karen."

So after that, every day, Sophie and I would say hello to the mulch of Karens scratching around in our backyard.

Then—seemingly overnight—the juncos left to go north for the summer. And I soon realized how much I missed them.

"I miss the juncos," I told Sophie one afternoon, as I was looking out the living-room window.

"Yeah," she said, and frowned. "No more Karen."

Sophie and I lamented the juncos' absence for a month or so. Then, as we were planning our trip to Oregon, I realized that juncos summer in Oregon. (Among the several subspecies of Dark-eyed Junco, one is actually called the Oregon Junco. The Slate-colored Junco is the subspecies that occupied our backyard in Texas.) Sophie and I decided that, on our trip, we would take a walk together one morning to find Karen. It would be like a reunion—a recovery of what had left us. We were looking forward to it.

But we never went on that walk. Instead, on our first day in Oregon, we stood in my sister's backyard—where she had dug a small pond under a fir tree—and my sister pointed at the Fake Metal Heron that was lying on the ground by the pond. She was explaining that she had staked the Fake Metal Heron by the pond, hoping to dissuade a real Great Blue Heron from coming to eat all the fish in her pond—but she was pretty sure that the

Fake Metal Heron was lying on the ground because the real Great Blue Heron had come and had fought the Fake Metal Heron, and had won—and now all her fish were gone. And at that moment, I saw a junco land on one of the low branches of the fir tree next to the pond. It was an Oregon Junco—different from the ones in Texas, but still a junco.

"Sophie!" I cried. "A junco!"

And Sophie cried, "Karen!"

And we celebrated the accidental success of our abbreviated quest with a high-five, as my sister smiled and said, "Who's Karen?"

Loss is a pit. Loss is a ghost. But loss is also a blessing. The feeling of loss testifies that we have experienced something special. It asks us to honor what we once had—a form of supplication by suffocation. To feel loss—to feel that crack in the chest, that catch in the throat, that slow thickness in the thighs—is to partake of a sacrament. It is confirmation that there are, in life, good things worthy of our time.

It is cliché to say that we don't appreciate what we've got until it's gone. But clichés become clichés because they're true. Loss is often much harder than we anticipate, precisely because we do not realize how special the thing is until we lose it.

But as Sophie and I discovered, sometimes, if you shift where you're sitting—if you *relocate* yourself—you will see new things. And sometimes, if you're lucky, you might just re-find something that looks an awful lot like the thing you had lost.

The Eastern Bluebird
Sialia sialis

> Hope is the hardest
> love we carry.
>
> – Jane Hirshfield

Parenting is hard.

Some people will say they don't believe in God because no God who is truly good would let bad things happen to people. But as parents, we know that we don't "let" bad things happen to our children. If we're doing our best to be good parents, then we do everything we can to *prevent* the bad things from happening. But parenting is hard. So, even though we tell our kids 16,301 times to stop chasing each other through the kitchen, still, one of them is going to knock out a tooth after running tooth-first into the kitchen counter. Because parenting is hard. And the only way to really prevent all the bad things from happening is to control *everything*. And we can't do this because— while controlling everything might help to prevent the bad things—we know that controlling everything would itself be a bad thing. So we have to let go. We have to just do our best, and then hope for the best.

This is basically what God does. God tells us 16,301 times not to run through the kitchen. And after we knock out a tooth on the kitchen counter, we respond by doubting God's existence.

As parents, we should have a lot more empathy for God.

Because parenting is hard.

***

The Pima believed that a flock of gray birds found a blue lake high in the mountains and bathed in the lake for four days. On the fourth day, they emerged from the lake with no feathers. But on the fifth day, their feathers grew back the same brilliant blue of the lake water. This is where bluebirds came from.

Bluebirds are native only to North America—and we have three varieties: the Eastern Bluebird, the Western Bluebird, and the Mountain Bluebird. The Mountain Bluebird has a whitish belly but is otherwise all blue—a light, bright blue that, in full bloom, is quite stunning. My guess is that the Pima had the Mountain Bluebird in mind when they told their story about the original blue birds.

The Eastern Bluebird and the Western Bluebird are both a deeper blue than the Mountain Bluebird, and they are almost identical. In the areas where their ranges overlap (mostly in New Mexico), they can be hard to tell apart. Each has a blue head, blue back, and blue wings, with a rust-colored breast. But sometimes that rust color will leak onto the back of the Western Bluebird, making it easier to distinguish from the Eastern.

Referring to the Eastern—the only bluebird that lives in New England—Henry David Thoreau famously wrote: "The bluebird carries the sky on its back." Considering the bluebird's rust-colored breast, Thoreau easily could have added "and the earth on its chest." But he didn't. So I'll say it:

> The bluebird carries
> the sky on its back and
> the earth on its chest.

Bluebirds are part of the thrush family (*Turdidae*), which means they're related to the Wood Thrush, Swainson's Thrush, the Varied Thrush, the Gray-cheeked Thrush, the Hermit Thrush, the Veery, and the American Robin. Most thrushes are varying shades of brown, with varying patterns of speckled-brown breasts. The robins and bluebirds—and the Varied Thrush—are the colorful exceptions.

Here in Collin County, the Eastern Bluebird is a somewhat common neighborhood bird. For a while, the nation's bluebird population was in decline due to suburban expansion and disappearing habitat. But the population has recently rebounded, thanks to bird lovers who have put nest boxes in their parks and backyards. So—fortunately—future generations will continue to see the beautiful blue bird that Thoreau once wrote poems about. The bird that carries the sky on its back, and the earth on its chest.

When our son Jackson was two years old, he would introduce himself to everyone as "Jackson Big Boy Steed." And when he was six, he would play Starfighter on the soccer field while all the other kids were learning to play soccer. The other six-year-olds would be on one end of the field, clumped in a collapsing mass around the soccer ball, and Jackson would be on the other end of the field, by himself, jumping and twisting and making laser-gun sound effects.

We asked him: "Jack, why aren't you with the other players? What are you doing when you jump around like that?"

And he answered: "I'm playing Starfighter."

We asked: "What's Starfigher?"

And he answered: "It's a single-player game I made up." As though this explained everything.

And now—suddenly—Jackson wants to study aerospace engineering at a big-boy university. He graduated from high school in May 2021. Our third child to leave the nest.

Soon after Jackson's graduation, I started seeing fledglings everywhere. For the birds, summer is the season of parenting. I saw Mallard ducklings on every pond, being guided to safety by their Mallard Moms. I watched Papa Barn Swallow feed his fledgling on a fence post. I watched a juvenile Red-tailed Hawk swoop in to perch near a parent—and then struggle to figure out which branch was strong enough to hold his weight.

And on several occasions, I watched a bluebird parent as it watched over its young'uns. Juvenile bluebirds don't look like their parents: they have spotty-brown chests and streaky, not-yet-blue backs. They won't carry the sky on their back or the earth on their chest until they reach adulthood. I would frequently see a mama or a papa bluebird with two or three young'uns, all perched along a fence, or along a roofline. And I would watch as the parents watched the young'uns learning to catch bugs on their own. Once in a while, the mama bluebird would hop down and grab a bug for herself—perhaps, in part, to model how it was done. But mostly the mama and the papa just sat back and watched, as the young'uns fumbled and flailed, trying to figure it out for themselves.

This is what we do, as parents. We try to teach our kids as best we can. We tell them 16,301 times not to run through the kitchen. We show them which pedal means go and which pedal means stop. We try to show them how to get food for themselves. But eventually, we have to just sit back and watch, as they fumble and flail. We can't control everything, or prevent all the bad things from happening. We can only do our best, and then hope for the best. And this, in itself, is its own special kind of hard thing.

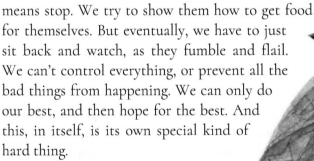

As parents, we carry the sky on our back and the earth on our chest. And we hope that we have taught our children well enough so that, one day, they will too.

The Sora
Porzana carolina

Some people never listen.

– Ernest Hemingway

After a successful trip to Oregon and Washington in July, our family felt okay about taking another trip in August—this time to Utah—when it was time to take Jackson to college. And after so much success at seeing new birds in the Pacific Northwest, I was excited about what I might see in the Intermountain West.

I wasn't disappointed.

After six days in Utah, my Life List leapt from 173 species to 190 species. I saw the Yellow-headed Blackbird, Townsend's Solitaire, the Western Grebe, the White-faced Ibis, the Caspian Tern, Woodhouse's Scrub-Jay, and Wilson's Snipe. I saw 42 species on a single morning at the Geneva Settling Ponds. And I took a hike up Battle Creek Canyon, which I later decided to rename Hummingbird Canyon because—although I didn't see much else—I saw dozens of hummingbirds all along the trail, including the Broad-tailed Hummingbird, the Calliope Hummingbird, and a shimmer of five Rufous Hummingbirds up at the top of the waterfall.

I also had an interesting experience that morning when I saw 42 species at the Geneva Settling Ponds. I'll tell you about that in a minute.

Did you know that in Japan they have a practice called *shin-rin yoku*, which means "forest bathing"? It's about immersing yourself in nature using all five senses. Florence Williams talks about it in her book, *The Nature Fix*. In her book (which I highly recommend), Williams makes a convincing case for spending more time in natural spaces. For starters, studies show that people walking in nature obsess over negative thoughts much less than people walking in cities. Leisurely forest walks—compared to urban walks—decrease cortisol levels 12%; decrease sympathetic nerve activity by 7%; decrease heart rate by 6%; and decrease blood pressure by 1.4%. Research shows that the stress of living in urban areas increases the odds of schizophrenia, anxiety, and mood disorders, while spending time in nature makes us healthier, more empathetic, and more focused and engaged. One study even showed a 50% increase in creativity after a few days in nature. And another study indicated that three days of hiking in the woods, for two hours a day, raised NK cell counts by 40%—a boost that lasted for a month! (NK cells are a kind of white blood cell that fights disease.)

Bottom line: when you get time off from work, don't go to a city. Go to a natural space—preferably one that is removed from the crowd, with lots of trees and water. And for good measure, you should go to a local park for a couple hours, at least once a week or so—in between vacations.

Williams talks about how, in *shinrin yoku*, people are serious about engaging *all* their senses when they interact with nature—so serious that they'll even chew bark or eat dirt, as they walk through the woods.

I admit I am less interested in this part of the practice. But I was very interested to learn about smells. I've always loved the smell of the grass and trees, after a heavy rain. And it turns out that forest smells are good for you. One study showed that three nights of sleeping with a humidifier filled with cypress oil can raise your NK cell count by 20%. And inhaling coniferous essential oils can lower cortisol levels and mitigate stress.

After reading this, I decided that—in addition to being a tree hugger—I would become a tree sniffer. So on my walks, every now and then, I would stop and hug a tree. First I would feel the girth of the tree in my arms. Then I would feel the scratchy bark against my cheek. Then I would tilt my nose and inhale deeply. I know this isn't exactly a scientific study—but I assure you: it does make me feel better. More grounded. More connected. Every time.

And I was even more interested to learn about sounds. Did you know that noise pollution—meaning "background" noise—is perhaps the most pervasive pollutant in the United States? Studies show that noise pollution affects reading comprehension, memory, and hyperactivity in children. For every increase of 5 decibels in one child's neighborhood, compared to another child's neighborhood, reading scores drop the equivalent of a two-month delay—meaning kids who live in noisy neighborhoods (20 decibels louder than comparable neighborhoods) are almost a year behind in their academic development, even after adjusting for other factors (like income). And noise pollution reaches nearly every corner of the country. According to the National Park Service, 83% of land in the lower 48 states is within 3,500 feet of a road—close enough to hear passing vehicles. By one researcher's count, there are fewer than a dozen sites in the country where, at dawn, you can go at least 15 minutes without hearing human-made noise. Even at Yosemite, you can hear aircraft flying overhead 70% of the time.

In an effort to create more quiet space—and a better connection to nature—Muir Woods (known for its redwoods) now has a "quiet zone" (soft voices, no phones, etc.). This has reduced background noise by three decibels. And every decibel matters. Three decibels is enough to effectively double the "listening area." In other words, instead of being able to hear birds that are chirping 10 yards away, you can hear birds that are chirping 20 yards away.

And by the way, did you know that—like tree smells—bird sounds are good for you? And good for society? Studies show that listening to birdsong will improve your mood and mental alertness. In 2011, the city of Lancaster, California, installed 70 speakers along its main street and piped in a chorus of bird sounds. The result? Minor crime fell by 15%, and major crime fell by 6%.

Conclusion: we need less noise and more birds. (It's worth noting that one of the side benefits of electric vehicles is that they're *quieter*.)

All this information in Williams' book really got my attention—especially the stuff about birdsong. By August, I had already begun to identify a lot of birds by sound. Or, to be more precise: by August I had become familiar with the sounds of a lot of the birds that I saw regularly—the Carolina Chickadee, the Northern Mockingbird, the Red-bellied Woodpecker, the Northern Cardinal, the Eastern Phoebe. I had seen these birds so many times that I didn't feel like I needed to *see* them before marking them on my daily list: if I heard them nearby, that was enough. And after reading *The Nature Fix* and learning about engaging with nature through all five senses, I not only started tree sniffing—I also started paying more attention to what I was hearing.

In 1992, the American Birding Association changed its official birding rules to allow for identifying birds by sound alone. (This was, in part, a move toward inclusivity—enabling those who are sight-impaired to participate more fully in the birding world.) I was not familiar with the ABA's birding rules during my first year of birding—but I had seen the movie *The Big Year*, in which Steve Martin's character mentions the acceptability of identifying a bird by ear. I had assumed the movie was 100% accurate and reliable, like all Hollywood movies—and I knew from experience that it was entirely possible to identify birds by sound, having done so myself many times. But so far, whenever I had identified a bird by sound, I had recorded it on my daily list only if it was a species I had *already previously seen.* Somehow, I didn't feel quite right about adding a new bird to my Life List that I had *only* heard and never actually seen.

For example, in Collin County, in the spring and summer, both the Red-eyed Vireo and the White-eyed Vireo are fairly common. But they both tend to stay high in the dense leafy treetops—where they're hard to see. I became expertly familiar with both birds' calls before I ever actually saw either one of them. But I didn't add either one to my Life List until I caught at least a fleeting glimpse.

But on the flipside, it's also worth noting that I couldn't properly identify some birds *until I heard them.* The Fish Crow looks essentially identical to the American Crow. So the best way to identify it is by sound—its nasally, understated *ow ow* being distinguishable from the American Crow's fuller and brasher *caw caw.* And then there are the flycatchers. The Alder Flycatcher and the Willow Flycatcher look so much alike that they used to be considered a single species (known as Traill's Flycatcher). They were split into two separate species only after ornithologists realized that they have different calls (and prefer slightly different habitats). The Alder calls *free-BEER,* and the Willow calls *FITZ-bew.* But visually, they remain almost identical. So the only sure way to identify them is by listening.

This reminds me of a wonderful phrase from the Quran, about how God's word is a reminder only for those who have a heart and for those who "throw their ears" (*alqa-ssam'a*)— meaning those who listen intently.

And then there's that old fable about the man who pleads, "God, please speak to me." And a meadowlark sings. But the man repeats his plea, not realizing it has been answered.

The first morning that I woke up in Utah, I went to the Geneva Settling Ponds. If you look on the map, the ponds are next to Vineyard Beach on Utah Lake, near Pleasant Grove—which is where we were staying. It's a great birding spot because there are gulls, terns, waterfowl, and shorebirds out on the lake, and herons, blackbirds, and a variety of songbirds around the ponds. Like I said, I saw 42 species that morning—which was, at that point, one of my highest totals ever.

As I walked around and between the ponds—which are surrounded with reeds and cattails, low brush and small trees—I heard lots of bird sounds: the machine gun *rat-a-tat-tat* of the Belted Kingfisher, the happy chatter of the Marsh Wren, the chips and chirps of House Finches, the light trill of a Yellow Warbler. I could identify all these birds by sound—and I had seen them all before—so I felt fine marking them on my morning's list, even though I hadn't yet caught sight of the wren or the warbler.

But then, as I neared the edge of one of the ponds, I heard something new. Among the piercing shrieks of the Yellow-headed Blackbirds, a single nasally *whee*—almost like a gull's cry—coming from deep in the thick reeds by the pond. Then a nasally descending *whee-hee-hee-hee-hee*. I pulled out my phone and opened my Merlin app to see if it could identify the sound. But of course, the bird went quiet. I crept slowly closer to the area where I thought the sound had come from. Then I stood there, leaning forward, whispering, "Do it again. Do it again."

It did it again. That nasally *whee*. I searched the reeds at the edge of the pond with my bare eyes, with my binoculars, with the camera lens. I couldn't see anything but reeds (and a small paddling of Mallards nearby). I started up the Merlin app again, hoping for another extended whinny. But silence. I crept a little closer to where I thought the bird was hiding.

I did this—crept around the pond, scanning the reeds and listening intently for that nasally *whee*—for 15–20 minutes. And it was probably the most intensely engaged 15–20 minutes that I had ever experienced on any of my walks—my eyes peeled and peering into the reeds, my ears straining for that sound, my thighs flexed in semi-crouch, my forearms poised with binoculars at the ready. It was exhilarating—the thrill of attentive anticipation.

But I never did see that bird. I heard it *whee* several more times. And I did manage to catch its nasally whinny on Merlin. Merlin identified it as the Sora. Which was exciting because the Sora was something entirely new to me. I kept trying to see it after Merlin identified it. But I never did. I could only relish its *whee*, each time I heard it.

The Sora is a type of rail, in the family *Rallidae*. The family includes birds like the Virginia Rail, the Clapper Rail, Ridgeway's Rail, and the King Rail, as well as the Common Gallinule, the Purple Gallinule, and the American Coot. The gallinules and coots are easier to see because they'll spend time out on the open water. And the American Coot was the only one of these birds that I had previously seen before that morning in Utah. I had seen many coots out on the water with the ducks, in the wintertime. But I had not realized that the coots were different from the ducks and mergansers until I started learning more about the Sora. It turns out that, as part of the rail family, the American Coot is more closely related to a crane than to a duck—with cranes being in the same order as rails (*Gruiformes*).

Unlike the coots and the gallinules, the rails can be hard to see. They spend most of their time on the shoreline—like the herons. And rails resemble herons a little bit, with their semi-long bills and semi-long legs. But the rails typically dwell deep in the brush or reeds instead of out on the open banks. Their bodies are even built more narrowly, making it easier for them to pass between the reeds.

Among the rails, the Sora is unique. At just 8–9" tall, it is roughly half the size of the other rails, with a shorter neck and a more bulbous shape. It also has a much shorter bill—more like the coot's—that turns bright yellow in adulthood. The Sora isn't as colorful and attractive as the Purple Gallinule. But in my opinion, it is much prettier than the other rails.

Of course, I know this only from the paintings and photos that I have seen in bird books and on my birding apps—because

I never did see that Sora at the Geneva Settling Ponds. It was just too small, and too deep in the reeds.

But I had heard it so distinctly, so many times—and my Merlin app had so readily identified its whinny—and my extended hunt for it had been such an intense, substantial, exhilarating part of my morning—that I decided to include the Sora on my list of the 42 species I had "seen" that day. It was the first time I had added a new bird to my Life List without actually seeing it. And I felt just fine about that.

When I got back in my car and started driving, that Josh Ritter song came up on my playlist, with those lines:

> Sometimes I can't see;
> that don't mean I'm blind.

And I took this as confirmation.

As of this writing, I still haven't seen the Sora—though I've heard it a few more times, in a few more places. And since that morning in Utah, when I didn't see the Sora, I have added a few more birds to my Life List that I didn't see—including the Least Bittern (*coo-coo-COO-coo*) and the Yellow-bellied Flycatcher (*tur-REE*).

The Sora opened me up to a new way of experiencing the world. I had heard lots of birds before I didn't see the Sora. But until I didn't see the Sora, I had never *only* heard the birds that I had been hearing. I had always seen them, too, at one time or another—and I had always relied on my eyesight to validate those earsounds. On my Life List—on the official record of all the birds that I have "seen"—the Sora became the first bird that I had identified and experienced *only* by listening. The first bird that I had seen without seeing.

To be sure, we all need to spend more time in nature. But the Sora taught me that we can't just "spend time" in nature. We need to *engage* with and immerse ourselves in the natural world. And to do this, we need to employ—and trust—*all* our senses. We need *shinrin yoku*. We need to feel the soft earth under our feet, the warm sun on our neck. See the mist glide over the lake and the varying shades of brown where the ground changes from firm soil to soft mud. Smell the woody perfume of treebark. And listen! We need to throw our ears and hear the *whee* of life, as it rises into the air from deep in the reeds.

The Great Blue Heron

Ardea herodias

Can you imagine us, years from today,
sharing a park bench quietly?

– Paul Simon

When I was in Oregon on that fateful trip that introduced me to Frankie, there was an afternoon when I was sitting around with my family, talking about animals. My brother-in-law, Ian, told a story about some elk he had seen on a hunting trip. Someone else—I think it was my brother Jon—recounted the time when the dogs had trapped a possum under the car. And I told everyone about George, the Great Blue Heron that I kept seeing on my walks through the neighborhood. At that time, I told my family the same thing that I've now told you: that George had become my friend, and that I looked forward to seeing him whenever I went out walking.

A short time after I returned to Texas, I received a surprise in the mail. My niece, Norah—Jon's daughter—had sent me a drawing she had done of George. Not a drawing, exactly, but a collage-like work of art. I fell in love with it immediately and put it in an 8x10 frame on my dresser. My own little portrait of George, watching over the shoes in my closet.

It was shortly after that, when I was looking at this portrait of George and thinking about some of my birding experiences, that I got the idea for this book: a book about what my encounters with birds had taught me about surviving the hard things. With artwork by Norah Steed.

***

In my past life, I was an English professor. (I left academia to go to law school in 2006.) As an English professor, I used to teach Oscar Wilde's play, *The Importance of Being Earnest*, in my "Introduction to Literature" classes. Then we would watch the movie version, starring Reese Witherspoon, Frances O'Connor, Rupert Everett, and Colin Firth. (The movie was still new back then, and it was a good way to make old literature seem new to my students.)

One night in 2021, I came across that movie on one of the streaming services that we use these days, and I decided to watch it. I hadn't been an English professor for 15 years, and I hadn't seen that movie for 16 years, and it was wonderful re-connecting with Wilde's witticisms. In *The Catcher in the Rye*, J.D. Salinger has this great line about how a good book is one that makes you "wish the author that wrote it was a terrific friend of yours and you could call him up on the phone whenever you felt like it." That's how I feel about *The Importance of Being Earnest*. Reconnecting with the play was like reconnecting with an old friend. I mean, the movie itself is just okay—not the greatest adaptation. But Wilde has some brilliant one-liners. You really need to read the play if you haven't already. Or go back and read it again, to reconnect.

And all this reminds me that Wilde had a great line about birds, too. He described nature as "a place where birds fly around uncooked."

Oh, Oscar. You old bean.

Herons like George are the stuff of legend. The Algonquin have a story about how Heron outsmarted Wolf. After hearing Weasel praise his stature, Heron helped Weasel across the river. Witnessing this, Wolf likewise praised Heron, saying, "I bet you are strong enough to help me across the river, too. For I am old and my bones ache." Heron said, "Sure, climb on my back and I will help you." Wolf congratulated himself, planning to eat

Heron on the other side. But halfway across, Heron stopped and said, "I was wrong: it will take the strength of two herons to carry you—you must find a second heron to take you from here." And Heron shook Wolf off his back and into the river, and flew away.

The image of Heron shaking Wolf from his back and flying away reminds me of those lines from a poem by Will Ogilvie, about a heron:

> Now he hears a footstep; wakes a sleeping power;
> Wide-winged and wonderful sails away, and slow.

In Ancient Greece, the heron was considered a messenger of the gods—often sent by Athena (the goddess of wisdom) or Aphrodite (the goddess of love). In *The Odyssey*, Athena sent a heron to Odysseus to let him know she was watching over him.

I've already told you about how important George was to me when I first started going for walks, just after the world shut down. And even when I started identifying other birds, I remained excited to see George throughout the fall and winter. When I saw him, I would say to myself, "There's George"—or sometimes I would even call out to him: "Hey George!"—and I would pause and watch him for a moment as he stepped slowly along the pond's edge.

But as spring approached—and then as spring passed and summer arrived—I sort of lost touch with George. I would still mark my tally whenever I saw him. But I no longer really *saw* him. I stopped saying his name out loud, and I stopped pausing to watch him. He had become that old friend who you used to hang out with all the time, and who you still see around now and then, but who you no longer talk to, for no particular reason other than drift.

***

In November 1991, I was turning 20 and living in Orono, Maine. (Why I was living in Maine is another story, for another time.) One night, I found myself staying overnight with a group of guys—some of whom I'd just met—and we stayed up late, talking about sports and life and other things that 20-year-olds might talk about. One guy and I hit it off. And as the others went to sleep, he and I continued talking till morning. His name was Paul—my dad's name, my middle name—and we talked about the similar experiences we had had in high school. We had both been skate-punks. We had both been bullied by the older boys. We shared war stories. We laughed a lot.

Paul and I became instant best friends. We didn't see each other very often because we were living in different New England towns, but we stayed close for about a year or so. Then I moved back west, and we drifted.

Four years later, in September 1996, Michele and I were one year into marriage, with a nine-month-old son, and we were living in Moscow, Idaho. And one Sunday morning, Paul came walking through the doors of our church with his new wife and their one-year-old son in tow. And the four of us—me-and-Michele and Paul-and-Tiffani—became inseparable. We saw each other five, six, sometimes seven days a week. Our sons, Cameron and Corbin, were best little buddies. Then we each had our second child—so Michele and Tiffani shared stories about pregnancy, while Paul and I shared stories about our pregnant wives. And we laughed a lot.

We were inseparable for three years—until Michele and I had to move away, and geography divided us. But we continued to keep in touch regularly for nearly 10 years, as Michele and I migrated from Idaho to Nevada, then to Oregon, then to Utah, then to Texas. We still saw each other at least once or twice a year—planning pit stops or detours during family trips, and sometimes planning special trips just to spend time together.

But when we moved to Texas, the distance was different. And we each had more kids. We were becoming *settled*. It got harder to make all those trips. And eventually, finally, some-time around 2008 or 2009, we drifted out of touch.

And then a decade passed. As time does.

Then one night in 2020, just as I was climbing into bed—not long before I would take that fateful trip to Oregon—I got a text from Paul. He was experiencing some hard things and he wanted me to know about it. I texted him back to tell him I was sorry to hear about the hard things, and I loved him. A couple days later, we talked on the phone. And it was as though no time had passed. My friend—my terrific old friend, with whom I had stayed up all night laughing on that night when we first met nearly 30 years ago—was still my terrific old friend who I could call up on the phone whenever I felt like it.

One hot morning in late August—after nearly a year of bird-ing and nearly a year of continuing to struggle through the hard things—I stumbled upon George at Summit View Lake. Sum-mit View is a neighborhood in McKinney, just north of 380, off Lake Forest Drive. Summit View Lake has a shallow marshy area near the dock—a favorite spot for herons. And one morn-ing I was walking past the playground, down toward that marshy spot—not being particularly quiet or careful—when I stumbled upon George just as he was stepping out of the reeds.

George had speared a fish, and the fish was stuck on the end of George's bill—stabbed through in two places because George's bill, apparently, had opened as he lunged. (He had probably meant to catch the fish in his open bill, but instead had speared it.) George had stepped out of the reeds and moved onto the grass and was shaking his head frantically—trying to shake the fish off his face. I froze and stifled a laugh. And I watched, transfixed by this comic scene. I finally remembered my camera, and raised it to get a photo. But George freed him-self before I could focus. And I watched as he picked up the limp fish, juggled it into position, and gulped it down.

I started to laugh again, softly, as he turned to stalk back in-to the reeds. And I said, "Good job, George." Then I broke into tears—suddenly overcome with gratitude for what I had just seen, and for all that I had experienced over the past year, since that first time I had watched George catching fish on the pond at Whitley Place. The morning when I first named him George.

Nothing is quite so wonderful as reconnecting with an old friend. Drift happens. Drift is normal. We all have at least one old friend from whom we've drifted. But thankfully, drift can be overcome. It takes only a text. A phone call. The slightest effort—and suddenly you're back together again. Laughing. As though no time has passed. Just you and your terrific old friend.

The Great Crested Flycatcher
Myiarchus crinitus

> may my heart always be open to little
> birds who are the secrets of living
>
> – e.e. cummings

My impression is that seasoned birders will tell you that summer is the worst time for birding. For one thing: it's hot. And in Texas, the heat is real. In July and August, it's often already in the high 80s at 6:00 a.m., and well into the 90s by 8:00. And it seems like the number of birds that come to stay for the summer (the herons, the swallows, the vireos, the flycatchers) is much lower than the number of birds that come for the winter (the kinglets, the thrushes, the finches, the sparrows—and all those waterfowl). But this was still my first year of birding, so summertime birding was still new and exciting to me.

Back when spring was approaching, I got excited about migration and about the arrival of all the warblers, buntings, swallows, hummingbirds, and vireos. I spent hours looking at the guidebooks—at all the blues, greens, oranges, and yellows that were to come. And don't get me wrong: migration is great. All the warblers, buntings, swallows, hummingbirds, and vireos are great. But as spring arrived and then warmed to summer, I found myself growing less excited about the warblers, buntings, swallows, hummingbirds, and vireos, and more enamored with the flycatchers—a family of much plainer-looking perchers. By July, I realized that the flycatcher family (*Tyrannidae*) had become one of my favorite families when—on our Oregon trip—I saw the Pacific-slope Flycatcher. When I saw the Sloper, with its mossy shade of green, its two bright wing bars, and its tiny white eye-ring—hawking bugs from the dead branch of a blackberry bush—I immediately declared that it was my new favorite flycatcher. But just as I said these words, I recalled the kingbirds, the phoebes, and the Scissor-tailed Flycatcher—and I realized I couldn't possibly pick a favorite. I realized that I loved *all* the flycatchers. And this surprised me.

Flycatchers aren't known for their melodious singing. Most of them don't really have a song—just a short, buzzy call, like the Eastern Phoebe's *FEE-bee* or the Willow Flycatcher's *FITZ-bew*. And they aren't known for their colorful, distinctive plumage, either. The Eastern Phoebe, the Acadian Flycatcher, the Alder Flycatcher, the Least Flycatcher, and the Willow Fly-catcher all have a grayish or olive-grayish head and back, with a mostly whitish throat and chest. In other words, these five little birds are all somewhat plain-looking—even drab, compared to the warblers and hummingbirds. And it can be extremely diffi-cult to tell them apart, especially for a beginning birder like me.

Because they aren't colorful—and because they are harder to differentiate—I had passed over the flycatchers when I was searching the guidebooks in anticipation of spring. But then, as spring arrived, I kept seeing them everywhere. I was already familiar with the Eastern Phoebe, which lives in Collin County year-round. But then the Acadian, Alder, Least, and Willow Flycatchers all came passing through during migration. I was seeing flycatchers all the time—but I couldn't always identify what I was seeing. It felt good when I was able to tell the phoe-bes from the not-phoebes. And it felt even better when I was able to differentiate the Least Flycatcher from the others. But I found the flycatchers challenging.

And then I discovered that this family also includes the Eastern Kingbird, the Western Kingbird, and the Scissor-tailed Flycatcher—all of which had come to stay for the summer. The kingbirds are both handsome, regal-looking birds. And the Scissor-tailed Flycatcher is a gorgeous tropical trophy bird—

with its white head, pinkish belly, and forked, foot-long tail feathers. The Scissor-tail is so stunningly beautiful that it is featured on the box of Wingspan—that board game that I was telling you about in the first chapter.

And I learned that, although most flycatchers aren't known for their singing or for their plumage, according to *Life of the Flycatcher* by Alexander F. Skutch, they *are* known for "the quality of their parental care"—as vigilant protectors of their young, and even as protective proxy parents to the young of other species. Skutch tells of a time when he watched a pair of Boat-billed Flycatchers in Central America, as they chased off a pair of much larger Chestnut-mandibled Toucans to prevent those huge-billed birds from plundering eggs from another bird's nest.

Seriously, the flycatchers are awesome. I love them. But I really didn't see that coming. And sometimes making new friends is like that. You really don't see it coming.

Like a lot of men, I don't have many close friends. A recent study found that only 27% of men have six or more friends that they would characterize as "close." Fifty-eight percent of men have only 1–5 close friends. And 15% have no close friendships at all. As I see it, there are the people you like when you see them at prescheduled events (such as work or church or your kid's dance recital); then there are the people for whom you actually schedule events—to see them—*because* you like them. There's a difference between these two groups of people. I would still call the first group "friends." But it is only the second group that has any chance of becoming "close friends." And, as I said—like most men my age, busy with career and family—I don't really have many close friends.

Not long after we moved to Prosper, I got invited to a "game night" by a guy named John, who I hardly knew. I don't remember why or how it happened. But in our area there's this small group of guys—sometimes only four or five, sometimes as many as eight or ten—who get together to play board games once a month. And somehow I got the email.

I've already told you that I like board games. So I went to game night a couple times. And it was fun. But then I couldn't go for a long period—when game night kept falling on a night when I was traveling for work, or busy with family activities, or otherwise somehow unavailable. Then COVID happened and game night didn't happen for a while.

But as the pandemic subsided and game night resumed, I started going more regularly. And soon I found myself going not primarily for the gameplaying, but instead to spend time with the guys. And we even started scheduling other times to hang out together—going to movies or to a Mavs game. One night, on the way to a Mavs game, we had a conversation about how hard it can be to make friends, or to *have* friends—and about how much we enjoyed spending time together.

And I realized that this small group of guys was approaching the label of "close friends." I'm sure we're a drab-looking bunch. And I really didn't see it coming. But I have to say, these game-night guys are pretty awesome.

As the summer wore on, I was not only surprised to realize that the somewhat-drab flycatchers had become one of my favorite families; I was also surprised to realize that the Great Crested Flycatcher had become one of my overall favorites.

The Great Crested Flycatcher is large for a flycatcher (7–9"). Instead of being grayish, like most of the flycatchers we see in Collin County, it has a richer brownish-greenish tone, with a copper streak in its wings and a yellow belly. And the Great Crested Flycatcher—who I nicknamed "G.C."—has a bold *wheep* that can be heard across the summer treetops.

I didn't see G.C. as often as I saw the kingbirds, the Eastern Phoebe, and the Scissor-tail. But—without realizing it at first—I started looking forward to seeing G.C. in the same way that I looked forward to seeing George. If George was my water friend, in the marshes and by the ponds and lakes, then G.C.

became my forest friend, in the woods and along the treelines. I would get excited every time I heard G.C.'s *wheep*—and even more excited when I caught sight of that fluffed crest poking out from the leaves.

One hot, late-August morning at Erwin Park, I stopped walking and sat down to watch four G.C.'s chasing each other through the branches and whooping it up, as the sun peeked over the treetops. And I realized it was a lot like that day when I watched George stab and struggle with that fish.

That same morning, as I was heading back toward the car, the cheap hiking boots that I had purchased the previous October expired. I mean, they literally fell off my feet: the sole of my left boot just...detached...and started flopping as I walked. On any other morning, I might've felt disappointment or frustration. But I had just watched G.C. playing tag. And I had sat there for some time, feeling the fullness of finding new friends. So when my boot fell apart, there was something oddly satisfying about it. Like I had accomplished something. So I just smiled, and chuckled, as I flopped my way back to the car.

Old friends like George are wonderful. But G.C. and the flycatchers reminded me that new friends can be wonderful too. Be open to meeting and loving new people. Be open to unplanned, unexpected new friendships. After all, new friends hold all the wonderful potential of becoming old friends.

Fall (again)

A Beginning

Can you picture what will be?
So limitless and free!

— Jim Morrison

The hero's journey is a walk through the neighborhood. It's a trip around the bases. You start from home, you go out into the world, and you come back home again—hopefully having gained something along the way. Yes, there will be losses along the way, too. That's part of the journey. Sometimes the only way to gain something is by losing something. Sometimes the breakthrough comes only after a breakdown. It's like the words of that old hymn by Sarah Adams:

> So by my woes to be
> nearer, my God, to thee.

Sometimes the hard things are what make it possible for us to glimpse the sublime—to experience the divine.

When Jacob, the son of Isaac, was afraid that his brother Esau was going to confront him with an army of 400 men and wipe him off the face of the earth, he prayed for deliverance. He made preparations. He sent gifts, hoping to slake Esau's anger. Then, the night before he was to meet his brother, a Man appeared. And Jacob wrestled with the Man. They struggled through the night. And when the Man saw that Jacob would not yield, the Man "touched the hollow of Jacob's thigh"—which is to say, the Man dislocated Jacob's hip. But still, Jacob would not yield.

Jacob said, "I will not let you go until you bless me."

And the Man said, "What is your name?"

And Jacob said, "My name is Jacob."

And the Man said, "Your name will no longer be Jacob, but Israel"—which means *one who wrestles with God.*

And Jacob, now Israel, said, "What is your name?"

And the Man said, "Why do you need to ask my name?"

And Israel knew that he had come face to face with God.

It was morning and Israel lifted his eyes and saw Esau, with his 400 men. And Israel bowed before Esau. And Esau ran to meet Israel and embraced him. And they wept together.

Legend has it that, for the rest of his life, Israel walked with a limp from that night when God dislocated his hip. But he also became the father of multitudes. The namesake of the House of Israel.

Israel's story is the story of wrestling with and surviving the hard things. When the hard things come, and the fear sets in, we pray for deliverance. We make preparations. We wrestle through the night—for however long the night lasts. And we rarely emerge from the struggle unharmed. There will be losses. The struggle will break some part of us. It will pull us apart. *Dislocate* us.

But if we hang on—if we do not yield—the morning will come. And with it, a new Self. Unavoidably, we will carry the scars and limps of that night-long struggle. But the scars and limps are our tokens. Our reminders. Our awkward trophies. They are part of what we keep—part of what we have gained from that night when God touched us.

I started this journey in the fall of 2020, after seeing the Pileated Woodpecker while walking in Oregon. A year later, having wrestled with hard things—and having, at times, been touched by God—I found myself back in Oregon visiting my parents again. One morning, as I sat in the back pasture on a fallen oak tree overlooking the hillside where I grew up, I thought about the birds I had seen and the things I had learned over the past year. And I decided I really needed to write this book. Even if it was only for me.

Over the prior weeks, the air had been thinning. The oaks and maples were colorfully announcing the death of old things. And as I jotted down some notes with a pen on my little notepad, I heard Frankie cackle from the woods nearby. It was still early. In a moment, I would continue my walk. I would go find that woodpecker. But before I continued, I lifted my eyes and looked out over the western horizon. I was still wrestling with some hard things, and it would take me a while to put what I had gained into words. But as I sucked the crisp morning air into my lungs, I felt a swell of fresh hope, and I thought of those words from another Stafford poem:

> What can anyone give you greater than now,
> starting here, right in this room, when you turn around?

I stood up and turned to go after Frankie. And I made a plan for the day ahead: after my walk, I would write some more notes for this book. Then later, in the afternoon, I would drive into town and go find myself a new pair of hiking boots.

Afterwords

Collective Nouns

The word *flock* comes from the Old English *flocc*, which meant "a group." It originally referred only to a group of humans. But in the 13th century it was extended to refer to a group of animals—like a flock of sheep. It became common as a collective noun for birds in the 19th century. Unfortunately, it has become so dominant as a term for a group of birds that we rarely hear any of the other alternatives. Yes, everyone knows that a group of crows is called "a murder of crows." But there are so many other collective nouns for birds that are so much more vivid than "flock"—and many of these terms have been around for 500 years.

Below is a list of collective nouns for many of the birds that are mentioned in this book. For each previously established collective noun, I've provided a source, and for those that I made up myself, I've provided page numbers for where they appear. If a bird is mentioned in this book but it doesn't appear on this list, that means I couldn't find a collective noun for that bird— and I didn't have an occasion to make one up.

By the way, as long as we're talking about collective nouns, I thought I'd mention a few of my favorite collective nouns from the legal world. They are:

- ❖ a quill of appellate lawyers
- ❖ a presumption of prosecutors
- ❖ a gavel of judges
- ❖ a deliberation of jurors

Okay, now back to the birds:

Bird	Noun	Source
Blackbirds	Racket	Pages 79, 84
Cardinals	Radiance	Lipton, *An Exaltation of Larks* (1991)
Coots	Cover	*The Book of St. Albans* (1486)
Cormorants	Gulp	Lipton, *An Exaltation of Larks* (1991); page 54
Crows	Murder[1]	*The Hors, Shepe & the Ghoos* (1476)
Doves	Pitying	Porkington MS (15th c.); page 107
Ducks; see also Mallards	Paddling (when on water) Team (when in flight)	Egerton MS (*circa* 1450); page 127
Finches; see also Goldfinches	Charm[2]	*The Book of St. Albans* (1486)

[1] Everyone knows this Hitchcockian noun for crows. But did you know about "an unkindness of ravens"? See *The Folk Lore of British Birds* (1885).

[2] This is presumed to be an error. That is, *The Book of St. Albans* (1486) refers to a "cherme" of finches—and later this was mistakenly transcribed as "charm." But authorities agree that *cherme* was actually a Middle English variant of the Old English *cirm*, which meant "noise, din, chatter." I think "a chatter of finches" works pretty well. But "a charm of finches" is delightful. So let's call it a happy accident. By the way, "a school of fish" also appears to have been a mistaken transcription. It was originally "a shoal of fish." See Lipton, *An Exaltation of Larks* (1991).

Bird	Noun	Source
Geese	Gaggle	*The Book of St. Albans* (1486); page 54
Goldfinches	Treasure[3]	Pages 67, 74
Gulls	Squabble	Lipton, *An Exaltation of Larks* (1991)
Herons	Siege	Egerton MS (*circa* 1450); page 5
Hummingbirds	Shimmer	Lipton, *An Exaltation of Larks* (1991); page 122
Jays	Gang[4]	Page 83
Juncos	Mulch	Page 116
Kinglets	Court	Page 18
Mallards	Flush	Egerton MS (*circa* 1450)
Owls	Parliament[5]	*The Book of St. Albans* (1486)

---

[3] *The Book of St. Albans* (1486) refers to a "cherme of goldefynches." But "charm" is also used to refer to finches more generically. (See prior entry for Finches.) So I decided to use "treasure" when referring to goldfinches —because I know how it feels to come around a bend and spy a treasure of goldfinches.

[4] The old sources say "party of jays." See Lipton, *An Exaltation of Larks* (1991). But—for reasons that I think are clear to anyone familiar with jays—I think "gang" is better.

[5] This is one of my favorite collective nouns. So perfect that I wish I had come up with it myself.

Bird	Noun	Source
Pigeons	Dropping	Lipton, *An Exaltation of Larks* (1991)
Siskins	Din	Page 177 (Footnote 44)
Sparrows	Host	*The Book of St. Albans* (1486)
Starlings	Murmuration	*The Hors, Shepe & the Ghoos* (1476)
Swallows	Flight	*The Book of St. Albans* (1486)
Thrushes	Mutation[6]	Porkington MS (15th c.)
Titmouses	Flute	Page 26
Warblers	Bouquet	Page 66
Waxwings	Candle	Page 43
Wrens	Herd[7]	*The Book of St. Albans* (1486)

---

[6] It was believed as recently as 1867 that thrushes lost their legs and grew new ones "when about 10 years old." See Lipton, *An Exaltation of Larks* (1991). I find this so bizarre.

[7] This was apparently considered an honorific, back in the day: one commentator observed that wrens were probably "allowed the term of 'herd'" because the wren was "the king of birds." See Lipton, *An Exaltation of Larks* (1991). But these days, "herd" is for livestock. So this is one I would change. If I had had the occasion to do so, I would've said something like "a chorus of wrens." If I had had occasion to do so, I also would've used "a passion of robins."

Lists & Numbers

First 200 Species by Date

10/01/2020	1. Pileated Woodpecker ("Frankie")
10/10/2020	2. Great Egret
	3. Black Vulture
	4. Eastern Phoebe
	5. Blue Jay
	6. Northern Mockingbird
	7. Northern Cardinal
10/12/2020	8. Mallard
10/13/2020	9. Great Blue Heron ("George")
10/14/2020	10. Common Grackle
10/16/2020	11. Mourning Dove
	12. Downy Woodpecker[8]
	13. American Crow
	14. Great Horned Owl
10/17/2020	15. Carolina Chickadee
10/18/2020	16. Red-tailed Hawk

---

[8] The Downy Woodpecker (Bird #12) was the first "new" bird I saw, after I officially started birding. As a new birder, I learned that the Black Vulture (Bird #3) is distinct from the Turkey Vulture (Bird #39); that the little gray bird I kept seeing near the pond was an Eastern Phoebe (Bird #4); and that the ubiquitous black birds that fill Walmart parking lots are called grackles (Bird #10). But I had seen all these birds (Birds #2–11) numerous times before I started birding—and, as mentioned, I had heard the Pileated Woodpecker (Bird #1) many times, growing up. So the Downy Woodpecker stood out as the first bird that was entirely new to me.

	17. Eastern Bluebird
	18. American Robin
	19. House Sparrow
10/20/2020	20. Canada Goose[9]
10/21/2020	21. Tufted Titmouse
	22. European Starling
	23. House Finch[10]
10/22/2020	24. Cooper's Hawk
10/23/2020	25. Red-headed Woodpecker ("Woody")
	26. Northern Flicker
10/25/2020	27. Ruby-crowned Kinglet
10/27/2020	28. Carolina Wren
10/29/2020	29. Killdeer
	30. Red-bellied Woodpecker
	31. Pine Siskin
	32. Yellow-rumped Warbler
10/30/2020	33. Pied-billed Grebe
	34. Rock Pigeon
	35. American Coot
	36. Scissor-tailed Flycatcher
	37. Eastern Meadowlark

---

[9] "Goose" is perhaps the oldest bird name that is still in use, dating back to over 5,000 years ago. Other bird names that are 1,000 years old—or older—include "gull," "ptarmigan," "redstart," "raven," and "crow."

[10] The House Finch's native range was limited to the Southwest until the 1940s. In 1940, pet dealers in New York City started selling House Finches (illegally) as pets, renaming them "Hollywood Finches." When U.S. Fish & Wildlife threatened prosecution, the pet dealers released all their birds, and those birds started a new East Coast population of House Finches that spread westward. By 1995, the House Finch's year-round range covered the entire United States. Today, it is probably our most common finch—and it is definitely the one I saw the most during my first year of birding. I must say, however, that its name is terrible. This is a gorgeous red bird that should be called something more descriptive—like the "Flame Finch" or the "Cherry Finch." Or—given its history—why not call it the "Hollywood Finch"? Anything would be better than the prosaic "House Finch."

11/01/2020	38. Yellow-bellied Sapsucker
11/02/2020	39. Turkey Vulture
	40. Great-tailed Grackle
11/03/2020	41. Ring-billed Gull
11/05/2020	42. Belted Kingfisher
	43. Dark-eyed Junco ("Karen")
11/07/2020	44. Blue-headed Vireo
	45. Brown Creeper
	46. White-throated Sparrow
11/08/2020	47. Brown Thrasher[11]
11/10/2020	48. American Wigeon
	49. Double-crested Cormorant
11/12/2020	50. White-winged Dove
	51. American Goldfinch
11/13/2020	52. Red-shouldered Hawk
11/14/2020	53. Ring-necked Duck
11/16/2020	54. Northern Shoveler
	55. Fox Sparrow
	56. Song Sparrow
	57. Red-winged Blackbird
11/20/2020	58. Cedar Waxwing
11/22/2020	59. Canvasback
	60. Lesser Scaup
11/24/2020	61. Hermit Thrush
11/25/2020	62. Field Sparrow
	63. Harris's Sparrow
	64. Lincoln's Sparrow
11/26/2020	65. Spotted Towhee
11/28/2020	66. Golden-crowned Kinglet

---

[11] I didn't have occasion to write about thrashers in this book. But Brown Thrashers are very beautiful—and they're beautiful singers. They're somewhat hard to spot because they tend to stay deep in the undergrowth, hidden by low branches, low shrubs, and piles of fallen leaves. I usually hear them first—not the sound of their singing but the sound of their feet thrashing around in the leaves. It often feels like an accomplishment when I'm able to spot one.

11/29/2020	67. Eurasian Collared-Dove
	68. White-crowned Sparrow
11/30/2020	69. Gadwall
	70. Bufflehead
12/07/2020	71. Orange-crowned Warbler ("Mabel")
12/10/2020	72. Savannah Sparrow
12/14/2020	73. Hooded Merganser
12/27/2020	74. Bewick's Wren
01/31/2021	75. White-breasted Nuthatch
02/01/2021	76. Lark Sparrow
02/15/2021	77. Greater Yellowlegs
02/18/2021	78. Green-winged Teal
02/21/2021	79. Northern Pintail
03/06/2021	80. Chipping Sparrow
03/15/2021	81. Brown-headed Cowbird
03/16/2021	82. Northern Rough-winged Swallow
03/18/2021	83. Cliff Swallow
03/21/2021	84. Osprey
	85. Barn Swallow
03/24/2021	86. Hairy Woodpecker
	87. Fish Crow
03/26/2021	88. Wood Duck
04/01/2021	89. Blue-winged Teal
	90. Yellow-throated Warbler
04/04/2021	91. Barred Owl[12]
04/05/2021	92. Black-chinned Hummingbird
04/06/2021	93. Purple Martin
04/08/2021	94. Green Heron

---

[12] This was one of the most exciting days in my first year of birding. An owl! In the wild! I was walking along, scanning the trees, when I saw a large shape near a tree trunk—not more than 20 yards away. The owl just sat there while I took a good look (and several good photos). It was a different experience from when I stood in my own backyard and saw the two Great Horned Owls flying from our roof. To this day, I've still had only a small handful of owl sightings, and this first sighting of the Barred Owl remains the best I've had so far.

	95. Eastern Kingbird
04/09/2021	96. Snowy Egret[13]
04/10/2021	97. Northern Harrier
	98. Blue-gray Gnatcatcher
04/12/2021	99. American Kestrel
04/13/2021	100. Ruby-throated Hummingbird
	101. White-eyed Vireo
04/15/2021	102. Franklin's Gull
04/20/2021	103. Greater Roadrunner[14]
04/25/2021	104. Chimney Swift
	105. Semipalmated Sandpiper[15]
04/27/2021	106. Nashville Warbler
04/28/2021	107. Great Crested Flycatcher ("G.C.")
04/30/2021	108. Yellow Warbler
05/02/2021	109. Mississippi Kite
	110. Least Flycatcher
	111. Western Kingbird
05/03/2021	112. Common Nighthawk
05/04/2021	113. Painted Bunting
05/08/2021	114. Spotted Sandpiper
	115. Cattle Egret
	116. Willow Flycatcher
05/12/2021	117. Swainson's Thrush

---

[13] I originally celebrated the Snowy Egret as Bird #100. But I didn't feel 100% confident that I had correctly identified a handful of birds on my list, so later I went back and deleted them. That dropped the Snowy Egret to #96 and made the Ruby-throated Hummingbird #100. But I didn't know the hummingbird was Bird #100 when I saw it, so I never properly celebrated it as such. I feel kind of bad about that.

[14] I first saw the roadrunner on the side of the road—after I had finished a walk at Erwin Park and was in my car, on my way home. I caught only a brief glimpse of it, as it ran under some roadside shrubs. And it was quite a while before I saw another one. But just recently, we saw one run through our backyard—and the whole family got pretty excited about it.

[15] This was my first sandpiper, and thankfully I got lots of good photos to help me identify it. Sandpipers—like gulls—are very hard to tell apart. I still struggle with them quite a bit.

05/14/2021	118. Common Yellowthroat
05/15/2021	119. Yellow-crowned Night-Heron
	120. Blackburnian Warbler[16]
05/22/2021	121. Red-eyed Vireo
05/23/2021	122. Alder Flycatcher
06/20/2021	123. Indigo Bunting
06/28/2021	124. Little Blue Heron
06/30/2021	125. Vaux's Swift
	126. Anna's Hummingbird
	127. Rufous Hummingbird
	128. Bald Eagle
	129. Red-breasted Sapsucker
	130. Western Wood-Pewee
	131. Steller's Jay
	132. California Scrub-Jay
	133. Black-capped Chickadee
	134. Bushtit
	135. Lesser Goldfinch
	136. Black-headed Grosbeak
	137. California Quail
	138. Wild Turkey
07/01/2021	139. Sharp-shinned Hawk
	140. Pacific-slope Flycatcher
	141. Chestnut-backed Chickadee
	142. Violet-green Swallow

---

[16] The first few times I reviewed and revised my Life List, I almost deleted the Blackburnian Warbler. I was at Summit View Lake and saw a flash of movement high in the tippy top of a willow tree. Even with my binoculars, I didn't get a very good look at it. But I knew I saw orange—I definitely saw orange. And the bird was the size and shape of a warbler, during warbler season. Using my bird guides, I guessed—by process of elimination—that it had to be the Blackburnian. But I didn't feel 100% sure about it. And I felt uneasy about keeping the bird on my list—until my second year of birding, when I got a good look at a Blackburnian Warbler while on a work trip to Indiana. I went to a park where there were lots of Blackburnian Warblers, and they were all in the tippy tops of the trees—just like the one I saw at Summit View Lake.

	143. Purple Finch
	144. Black-throated Gray Warbler
	145. Wilson's Warbler
07/02/2021	146. Cinnamon Teal
	147. Tree Swallow
	148. Marsh Wren
	149. Brewer's Blackbird
	150. Western Gull
	151. Brown Pelican
	152. Warbling Vireo
07/06/2021	153. Black-billed Magpie
	154. Common Raven
	155. Mountain Chickadee
	156. Red-breasted Nuthatch
	157. Pygmy Nuthatch
	158. Red Crossbill
07/07/2021	159. Canyon Wren
	160. Gray Catbird[17]
07/08/2021	161. Red-naped Sapsucker
	162. House Wren
	163. Western Bluebird
	164. Veery
	165. Bullock's Oriole
07/15/2021	166. Yellow-billed Cuckoo[18]
07/18/2021	167. Orchard Oriole

---

[17] It's called a "catbird" because it really does make noises like a cat's *meow*.

[18] The cuckoo is notoriously hard to see. During the summertime, when you want to see birds in the trees and all the leaves are full, you rely heavily on larger sizes, brighter colors, or some kind of movement. A small, drab, stationary bird is almost invisible. The cuckoo isn't particularly small—it's about the size of a Blue Jay, with a longer tail. But it *is* relatively plain looking, and it tends to stay put. So it is heard more often than seen. If you hear one, try to get underneath the sound. The underside of the cuckoo's tail has bold black-and-white bars. So—if you can get underneath the sound and look up—you might spy the cuckoo's long black-and-white tail extending out over a branch.

	168. Dickcissel
08/09/2021	169. Least Sandpiper
	170. Long-billed Dowitcher
	171. White Ibis
08/13/2021	172. Loggerhead Shrike
08/16/2021	173. Swainson's Hawk
	174. Black-necked Stilt
08/23/2021	175. Western Grebe
	176. Sora
	177. Wilson's Phalarope
	178. California Gull
	179. Caspian Tern
	180. American White Pelican
	181. Black-crowned Night-Heron
	182. White-faced Ibis
	183. Bank Swallow
	184. Townsend's Solitaire
	185. Yellow-headed Blackbird
	186. Woodhouse's Scrub-Jay
08/24/2021	187. Calliope Hummingbird
	188. Broad-tailed Hummingbird
08/25/2021	189. Sandhill Crane
	190. Wilson's Snipe
	191. Black Phoebe
08/30/2021	192. Olive-sided Flycatcher
08/31/2021	193. Baltimore Oriole
09/05/2021	194. Eastern Wood-Pewee
09/06/2021	195. American Avocet[19]
09/08/2021	196. Lesser Yellowlegs
	197. Tricolored Heron
09/17/2021	198. Anhinga[20]

---

[19] I'm not a huge fan of the seabirds and shorebirds—I'm more of a riparian- and forest-birds kind of guy. But with its beautiful sunset coloring and its upturned bill, the avocet is one of my favorite shorebirds.

| 10/15/2021 | 199. Clay-colored Sparrow |
| 10/21/2021 | 200. American Pipit[21] |

First 200 Birds by Location

My Parents' Home (Monmouth, OR)	1. Pileated Woodpecker
	137. California Quail
	138. Wild Turkey
	139. Sharp-shinned Hawk
	140. Pacific-slope Flycatcher
	141. Chestnut-backed Chickadee
	142. Violet-green Swallow
	143. Purple Finch
	144. Black-throated Gray Warbler
	145. Wilson's Warbler

| Whitley Place (Prosper, TX)[22] | 2. Great Egret |
| | 3. Black Vulture |

---

[20] I originally celebrated the Anhinga as Bird #200. But when I revised my list, the same fate that befell the Snowy Egret (see Footnote 13) befell the Anhinga, and it dropped to #198. (See Footnote 21.)

[21] Technically, I saw the pipit about a week or so *after* I officially completed my first year of birding. I saw Frankie (Bird #1) on October 1, 2020, and I saw the Anhinga—which I thought was Bird #200 when I saw it—on September 17, 2021. So I thought I had seen exactly 200 birds, from October 1 to October 1. But then I reviewed and revised my Life List (again), and the Anhinga dropped (again) to #199. To even things out, I extended my first year to October 15—the day I saw the Clay-colored Sparrow—and at that point, I officially called an end to my first year of birding, having seen 200 birds from October 1 to October 15. The pipit became Bird #201 on October 21. But as I was writing this book, I reviewed my list (yet again) and deleted another bird, which dropped the pipit into the #200 spot. This single October 21 tally for the pipit is the only tally that falls outside the October-1-to-October-15 period. But we can still say that I reached 200 birds in my first year if we say the year ran from October through October—right?

4. Eastern Phoebe
5. Blue Jay
6. Northern Mockingbird
7. Northern Cardinal
8. Mallard
9. Great Blue Heron
10. Common Grackle
11. Mourning Dove
12. Downy Woodpecker
13. American Crow
15. Carolina Chickadee
16. Red-tailed Hawk
17. Eastern Bluebird
18. American Robin
19. House Sparrow
20. Canada Goose
21. Tufted Titmouse
22. European Starling
23. House Finch
24. Cooper's Hawk
25. Red-headed Woodpecker
26. Northern Flicker
27. Ruby-crowned Kinglet
28. Carolina Wren
32. Yellow-rumped Warbler
38. Yellow-bellied Sapsucker
40. Great-tailed Grackle
41. Ring-billed Gull
42. Belted Kingfisher

---

[22] Because our neighborhood is where I took most of my morning walks for the first couple months, it's where I saw the largest portion of my first 200 birds. These days, I no longer walk through our neighborhood very often—I prefer going to the woodsier parks with unpaved trails, or finding new locations to explore. But occasionally I'll revisit the neighborhood nature path. And so far, I have seen 113 bird species right here in Whitley Place. That's not too shabby.

43. Dark-eyed Junco
44. Blue-headed Vireo
45. Brown Creeper
46. White-throated Sparrow
50. White-winged Dove
51. American Goldfinch
66. Golden-crowned Kinglet
75. White-breasted Nuthatch
77. Greater Yellowlegs
78. Green-winged Teal
88. Wood Duck
92. Black-chinned Hummingbird
96. Snowy Egret
100. Ruby-throated Hummingbird
101. White-eyed Vireo
102. Franklin's Gull
107. Great Crested Flycatcher
112. Common Nighthawk
114. Spotted Sandpiper
115. Cattle Egret
116. Willow Flycatcher
117. Swainson's Thrush
121. Red-eyed Vireo
193. Baltimore Oriole
194. Eastern Wood-Pewee

My Home[23]   14. Great Horned Owl
(Prosper, TX)   71. Orange-crowned Warbler
                 74. Bewick's Wren
                 118. Common Yellowthroat

---

[23] As of this writing, I have seen 40 species of birds from our house (including birds flying overhead). And during my first year, I saw 31 species around our home, including the four listed here that I saw for the first time in our backyard. So be sure to look out your window!

Bonnie Wenk Park (McKinney, TX)	29. Killdeer
	30. Red-bellied Woodpecker
	31. Pine Siskin
	33. Pied-billed Grebe
	39. Turkey Vulture
	52. Red-shouldered Hawk
	58. Cedar Waxwing
	73. Hooded Merganser
	82. Northern Rough-winged Swallow
	86. Hairy Woodpecker
	87. Fish Crow
	91. Barred Owl
	106. Nashville Warbler
	123. Indigo Bunting
Pond on 380 (McKinney, TX)	34. Rock Pigeon
	35. American Coot
	36. Scissor-tailed Flycatcher
	37. Eastern Meadowlark
	48. American Wigeon
	49. Double-crested Cormorant
Town Lake Park[24] (Prosper, TX)	47. Brown Thrasher
	53. Ring-necked Duck
	54. Northern Shoveler
	55. Fox Sparrow
	56. Song Sparrow
	57. Red-winged Blackbird
	59. Canvasback
	60. Lesser Scaup
	67. Eurasian Collared-Dove

---

[24] As I've mentioned, Town Lake is one of my very favorite places to go. Unfortunately, I think they're planning to develop the backside of the lake into another suburban neighborhood. The main park area will remain—but I'm not sure all the birds will. And that is heartbreaking.

68. White-crowned Sparrow

72. Savannah Sparrow

79. Northern Pintail

84. Osprey

85. Barn Swallow

89. Blue-winged Teal

90. Yellow-throated Warbler

97. Northern Harrier

98. Blue-gray Gnatcatcher

104. Chimney Swift

105. Semipalmated Sandpiper

113. Painted Bunting

122. Alder Flycatcher

124. Little Blue Heron

167. Orchard Oriole

168. Dickcissel

192. Olive-sided Flycatcher

198. Anhinga

199. Clay-colored Sparrow

Erwin Park[25]
(McKinney, TX)

61. Hermit Thrush

62. Field Sparrow

63. Harris's Sparrow

64. Lincoln's Sparrow

65. Spotted Towhee

76. Lark Sparrow

80. Chipping Sparrow

103. Greater Roadrunner

166. Yellow-billed Cuckoo

---

[25] Erwin Park can get crowded with campers and mountain-bikers on the weekends, so it's best to go on a weekday morning. In January 2022, at the start of my second year of birding, I photographed a pair of Solitary Sandpipers that had decided to spend the winter at Erwin Park's pond—which was unusual, because Solitary Sandpipers usually winter in Mexico. This became my first confirmed sighting of a "rarity."

Nora Haney Park (McKinney, TX)	69. Gadwall
	70. Bufflehead
	83. Cliff Swallow
	94. Green Heron
	95. Eastern Kingbird
	173. Swainson's Hawk
Summit View Lake (McKinney, TX)	81. Brown-headed Cowbird
	93. Purple Martin
	108. Yellow Warbler
	119. Yellow-crowned Night-Heron
	120. Blackburnian Warbler
Park by Toyota[26] (Allen, TX)	99. American Kestrel
Frisco Commons (Frisco, TX)	109. Mississippi Kite
	110. Least Flycatcher
	111. Western Kingbird
Cook Park[27] (Tigard, OR)	125. Vaux's Swift
	126. Anna's Hummingbird
	127. Rufous Hummingbird
	128. Bald Eagle
	129. Red-breasted Sapsucker

---

[26] I took our car to the dealership one morning and, instead of waiting in the lobby, decided to go for a walk. Behind the dealership, I discovered a patch of undeveloped land adjacent to a neighborhood that has a pond with a walking path around it. The undeveloped land had two spillways, one on each side of the road. And on that first visit, I saw 28 species—including Wood Ducks and herons in the spillways, and an American Kestrel (a new lifer!) perched on a telephone wire. Now, every time I take my car in for maintenance, I head to this spot to see what I can see.

[27] Cook Park is fantastic. I saw 28 species when I went there—including the 12 new ones listed here—and I got lots of great photos. The park is gorgeous. And it's the sort of place where I'm sure it's possible to see 30–40 species, depending on the time of year. I can't wait to go back.

130. Western Wood-Pewee
131. Steller's Jay
132. California Scrub-Jay
133. Black-capped Chickadee
134. Bushtit
135. Lesser Goldfinch
136. Black-headed Grosbeak

Basket Slough[28] 146. Cinnamon Teal
(Polk County, OR) 147. Tree Swallow
148. Marsh Wren
149. Brewer's Blackbird

Road's End 150. Western Gull
State Park 151. Brown Pelican
(Lincoln City, OR) 152. Warbling Vireo

Steve & Tango's 153. Black-billed Magpie
Home 154. Common Raven
(Spokane, WA) 155. Mountain Chickadee
156. Red-breasted Nuthatch
157. Pygmy Nuthatch
158. Red Crossbill

Indian Painted Rock[29] 159. Canyon Wren
(Spokane, WA) 160. Gray Catbird
161. Red-naped Sapsucker

---

[28] Basket Slough is my favorite place to go whenever I'm visiting family in Oregon. It's a huge nature preserve, with lots of different areas to explore. Lately, the Morgan Lake area has been my favorite. But no matter which side of the preserve you're on, it'll be worth the trip.

[29] Painted Rock is one of my all-time favorite places. The trail is amazing, with a small mountain on your right and a river on your left. I've been up the trail three separate times now, and in addition to seeing 30–40 species of birds every time, I've also seen marmots, chipmunks, deer, and even a moose. I can't wait to go back again.

162. House Wren
163. Western Bluebird
164. Veery
165. Bullock's Oriole

Continental Ave.	169. Least Sandpiper
Pedestrian Bridge	170. Long-billed Dowitcher
(Dallas, TX)[30]	171. White Ibis
	172. Loggerhead Shrike
	195. American Avocet
	196. Lesser Yellowlegs
	197. Tricolored Heron
	200. American Pipit
Trammel Crow Park	174. Black-necked Stilt
(Dallas, TX)	
Geneva Settling Ponds	175. Western Grebe
& Vineyard Beach	176. Sora
(Vineyard, UT)	177. Wilson's Phalarope
	178. California Gull
	179. Caspian Tern
	180. American White Pelican
	181. Black-crowned Night-Heron
	182. White-faced Ibis
	183. Bank Swallow
	184. Townsend's Solitaire
	185. Yellow-headed Blackbird

---

[30] This bridge is on the west side of downtown Dallas, just minutes from my office, and it has become my favorite nearby place to go birding whenever I'm downtown. The wetland portion dried up in 2022 (when we had less rain and a hot summer), so there weren't as many herons and shorebirds. But the wetland portion came back in 2023—and on my last visit I saw 36 species.

Brian & Heidi's Home (Pleasant Grove, UT)	186. Woodhouse's Scrub-Jay
Battle Creek Falls[31] (Pleasant Grove, UT)	187. Calliope Hummingbird 188. Broad-tailed Hummingbird
Utah Lake State Park[32] (Provo, UT)	189. Sandhill Crane 190. Wilson's Snipe 191. Black Phoebe

First 200 Birds by Taxonomy

Ducks, Geese & Swans	8. Mallard
	20. Canada Goose
	48. American Wigeon
	53. Ring-necked Duck
	54. Northern Shoveler
	59. Canvasback
	60. Lesser Scaup
	69. Gadwall
	70. Bufflehead
	73. Hooded Merganser
	78. Green-winged Teal
	79. Northern Pintail
	88. Wood Duck
	89. Blue-winged Teal

---

[31] As mentioned, I saw *tons* of hummingbirds when I first went up this trail, especially around the waterfall itself. I've been back just once since then—at a different time of year—and I didn't see much. So the jury's still out on whether it deserves to be renamed "Hummingbird Trail."

[32] Although I first saw the Yellow-headed Blackbird at the Geneva Settling Ponds, I saw more of them—and got a much better look at them—in the reeds along the Provo River at Utah Lake State Park. If you're ever in Utah County, I recommend visiting both spots.

146. Cinnamon Teal

Gamebirds   137. California Quail
             138. Wild Turkey

Grebes   33. Pied-billed Grebe
          175. Western Grebe

Pigeons & Doves   11. Mourning Dove
                   34. Rock Pigeon
                   50. White-winged Dove
                   67. Eurasian Collared-Dove

Cuckoos & Roadrunners   103. Greater Roadrunner
                         166. Yellow-billed Cuckoo

Goatsuckers[33]   112. Common Nighthawk

Swifts   104. Chimney Swift
          125. Vaux's Swift

Hummingbirds   92. Black-chinned Hummingbird
                100. Ruby-throated Hummingbird
                126. Anna's Hummingbird
                127. Rufous Hummingbird
                187. Calliope Hummingbird
                188. Broad-tailed Hummingbird

---

[33] Most goatsuckers—including the Common Nighthawk—are nocturnal. In the summer, I usually see the nighthawks at dawn or dusk, swooping over the elementary school in our neighborhood, eating bugs in midair. The name "goatsucker" comes from the folktale that these birds feed on goat milk under the cover of darkness. This isn't true, of course. A better name (coined by Mike Toms) would be "mothgobbler." See *Mrs. Moreau's Warbler*, by Stephen Moss.

Rails, Gallinules & Coots	35. American Coot
	176. Sora
Cranes	189. Sandhill Crane
Avocets & Stilts	174. Black-necked Stilt
	195. American Avocet
Sandpipers & Phalaropes	29. Killdeer
	77. Greater Yellowlegs
	105. Semipalmated Sandpiper
	114. Spotted Sandpiper
	169. Least Sandpiper
	170. Long-billed Dowitcher
	177. Wilson's Phalarope
	190. Wilson's Snipe
	196. Lesser Yellowlegs
Gulls, Terns & Skimmers[34]	41. Ring-billed Gull
	102. Franklin's Gull
	150. Western Gull
	178. California Gull
	179. Caspian Tern
Cormorants	49. Double-crested Cormorant
Darters[35]	198. Anhinga

---

[34] So far, I think gulls are the hardest birds to distinguish by species. There are a few that stand out—like Franklin's gull, with its black head. But mostly they all look alike to me. For identification purposes, I rely heavily on range maps, leg color, and the Merlin Sound ID app.

[35] There are four species of darter and they are all named for where they live. The Anhinga (also known as the "American Darter") lives here in North America. The other three species are the African Darter, the Indian Darter, and the Australian Darter. All four are in the genus *Anhinga* and the American Darter is considered the "type species" (taxonomically

Pelicans	151. Brown Pelican
	180. American White Pelican
Bitterns, Herons & Egrets	2. Great Egret
	9. Great Blue Heron
	94. Green Heron
	96. Snowy Egret
	115. Cattle Egret
	119. Yellow-crowned Night-Heron
	124. Little Blue Heron
	181. Black-crowned Night-Heron
	197. Tricolored Heron
Ibises & Spoonbills	171. White Ibis
	182. White-faced Ibis
Vultures	3. Black Vulture
	39. Turkey Vulture
Ospreys	84. Osprey
Kites, Eagles & Hawks	16. Red-tailed Hawk
	24. Cooper's Hawk
	52. Red-shouldered Hawk
	97. Northern Harrier
	109. Mississippi Kite[36]
	128. Bald Eagle
	139. Sharp-shinned Hawk
	173. Swainson's Hawk

---

known as *Anhinga anhinga*). This is why the American Darter is also called, simply, the Anhinga.

[36] I would like to see more kites. I once saw five Mississippi Kites together at Bonnie Wenk Park. And in my second year of birding I saw the Swallow-tailed Kite, in the Houston area. But I still want to see more.

Owls	14. Great Horned Owl
	91. Barred Owl

| Kingfishers | 42. Belted Kingfisher[37] |

Woodpeckers	1. Pileated Woodpecker
	12. Downy Woodpecker
	25. Red-headed Woodpecker
	26. Northern Flicker
	30. Red-bellied Woodpecker
	38. Yellow-bellied Sapsucker
	86. Hairy Woodpecker
	129. Red-breasted Sapsucker
	161. Red-naped Sapsucker

| Caracaras & Falcons | 99. American Kestrel |

Flycatchers	4. Eastern Phoebe
	36. Scissor-tailed Flycatcher
	95. Eastern Kingbird
	107. Great Crested Flycatcher
	110. Least Flycatcher
	111. Western Kingbird
	116. Willow Flycatcher
	122. Alder Flycatcher
	130. Western Wood-Pewee

---

[37] Kingfishers are one of my favorites. I used to see them as a kid, in Oregon, while fishing or canoeing. They fly pretty fast, and they're usually flying—swooping and dipping and diving—so it's often hard to get a good look at them. But one time I was out in my kayak on Summit View Lake, and I saw a female kingfisher perched in a small tree on the back half of the lake (the part that bends around so you can't see it from the dock). She just sat there in the tree for a long time—so I just sat there in my kayak for a long time, watching her. It was great, and it remains the best look at a kingfisher I've ever had.

190. Pacific-slope Flycatcher
191. Black Phoebe
192. Olive-sided Flycatcher
194. Eastern Wood-Pewee

Shrikes	172. Loggerhead Shrike

Vireos	44. Blue-headed Vireo
	101. White-eyed Vireo
	121. Red-eyed Vireo
	152. Warbling Vireo

Crows & Jays	5. Blue Jay
	13. American Crow
	87. Fish Crow
	131. Steller's Jay
	132. California Scrub-Jay
	153. Black-billed Magpie
	154. Common Raven
	186. Woodhouse's Scrub-Jay

Swallows	82. Northern Rough-winged Swallow
	83. Cliff Swallow
	85. Barn Swallow
	93. Purple Martin
	142. Violet-green Swallow
	147. Tree Swallow
	183. Bank Swallow

Titmouses & Chickadees	15. Carolina Chickadee
	21. Tufted Titmouse
	133. Black-capped Chickadee
	141. Chestnut-backed Chickadee
	155. Mountain Chickadee

Bushtits	134. Bushtit
Nuthatches[38]	75. White-breasted Nuthatch
	156. Red-breasted Nuthatch
	157. Pygmy Nuthatch
Creepers[39]	45. Brown Creeper
Wrens	28. Carolina Wren
	74. Bewick's Wren
	148. Marsh Wren
	159. Canyon Wren[40]
	162. House Wren
Gnatcatchers	98. Blue-gray Gnatcatcher
Kinglets	27. Ruby-crowned Kinglet
	66. Golden-crowned Kinglet
Thrushes	17. Eastern Bluebird
	18. American Robin

---

[38] Nuthatches were once called "nut jobbers." This derived from a now-obsolete use of the word *job* to mean "peck" or "jab." And the suffix to the modern name (*-hatch*) derives from the word "hack," which refers to the bird's habit of pressing nuts into bark crevices and then hacking at them to break off edible pieces. Wouldn't it be great if we called them "nuthacks"?

[39] Like the Osprey and the Bushtit, the Brown Creeper is in a family of one. In appearance, it has some similarity to the wrens—and in behavior, it's a little like the nuthatches. The most interesting thing about the creeper, though, is that it won't turn upside down on a tree trunk like the nuthatch will—and it won't move backwards like a woodpecker. The creeper will face only upward, and it will move only forward. So, if you spot one, you can watch it work its way up the tree, then fly to the bottom of a neighboring tree to work its way up that one, and so on.

[40] The wrens are great singers, and the Canyon Wren is probably my favorite wren, partly for its song.

61. Hermit Thrush
117. Swainson's Thrush
163. Western Bluebird
164. Veery
184. Townsend's Solitaire

Mockingbirds & Thrashers
6. Northern Mockingbird
47. Brown Thrasher
160. Gray Catbird

Starlings
22. European Starling

Waxwings
58. Cedar Waxwing

Old World Sparrows
19. House Sparrow[41]

Wagtails & Pipits
200. American Pipit

Finches
23. House Finch
31. Pine Siskin
51. American Goldfinch
135. Lesser Goldfinch
143. Purple Finch
158. Red Crossbill

Blackbirds
10. Common Grackle
37. Eastern Meadowlark

---

[41] The House Sparrow is a European bird that was brought to Brooklyn in the 1850s. It was touted as a natural control for agricultural pests, and by the 1870s people were shipping crates of House Sparrows all over the country. At the time, ornithologists were debating the wisdom of this move. And today, the House Sparrow is widely considered an invasive species—and a pest—because it will take over nesting sites and crowd out other species. We had a pair of Eastern Bluebirds that tried to nest in our backyard, but they were muscled out by House Sparrows. I was *not* happy about that.

40. Great-tailed Grackle
57. Red-winged Blackbird
81. Brown-headed Cowbird
149. Brewer's Blackbird
165. Bullock's Oriole
167. Orchard Oriole
185. Yellow-headed Blackbird
193. Baltimore Oriole

Warblers
32. Yellow-rumped Warbler
71. Orange-crowned Warbler
90. Yellow-throated Warbler
106. Nashville Warbler
108. Yellow Warbler
118. Common Yellowthroat
120. Blackburnian Warbler
144. Black-throated Gray Warbler
145. Wilson's Warbler

Cardinals & Tanagers
7. Northern Cardinal
113. Painted Bunting
123. Indigo Bunting
136. Black-headed Grosbeak
168. Dickcissel

New World Sparrows
& Towhees
43. Dark-eyed Junco
46. White-throated Sparrow
55. Fox Sparrow
56. Song Sparrow
62. Field Sparrow
63. Harris's Sparrow
64. Lincoln's Sparrow
65. Spotted Towhee
68. White-crowned Sparrow
72. Savannah Sparrow
76. Lark Sparrow

80. Chipping Sparrow
199. Clay-colored Sparrow

First 200 Birds by "Most Seen"

A quick word about how I counted birds during my first year of birding: I didn't. That is, I didn't count the number of individual birds that I was seeing. I was interested only in the number of *species* that I was seeing. So instead of counting individual birds, I just marked a single tally for each species that I saw on a given day in a particular location. For example: if I went for a walk at Erwin Park on August 7, and I saw the Northern Cardinal, it didn't matter if I saw two cardinals at the start of my walk and six more at the end. If I saw the Northern Cardinal (the species), then I marked a single tally for the Northern Cardinal at Erwin Park on August 7. This became my "daily tally."

For the most part, my daily tally provides a record of the number of species I saw on a particular day, as well as a record of the number of days on which I saw a given species. But it isn't quite that simple because—while I didn't go for a walk every single day—on some days I went walking more than once. And my daily tally was tied not just to the day itself, but also to the location where I went walking—because I wanted to keep a record of the number of times that I saw a species *at that location*. So, if I saw the Northern Cardinal on my morning walk at Erwin Park, and I saw the Northern Cardinal again on an afternoon walk through my neighborhood, then I would end up with two tallies for the Northern Cardinal that day: one for Erwin Park, and another for Whitley Place. And eventually I started keeping a daily tally for our backyard, too.

This is how, after one year of birding (roughly 365 days), the Northern Cardinal ended up with 426 tallies.

Tally

426	7. Northern Cardinal
360	6. Northern Mockingbird[42]
301	11. Mourning Dove
250	23. House Finch
241	15. Carolina Chickadee
234	5. Blue Jay
214	8. Mallard
212	13. American Crow
200	30. Red-bellied Woodpecker
191	9. Great Blue Heron ("George")
174	43. Dark-eyed Junco[43] ("Karen")
170	28. Carolina Wren
163	32. Yellow-rumped Warbler
159	12. Downy Woodpecker
152	21. Tufted Titmouse
152	85. Barn Swallow
144	4. Eastern Phoebe
132	2. Great Egret
132	17. Eastern Bluebird
124	18. American Robin
121	31. Pine Siskin[44]

---

[42] The Northern Mockingbird is not as common as the Northern Cardinal. But it has been perhaps the most common visitors to our backyard.

[43] Some birds' tallies are heavily padded by the number of times they showed up in our backyard. The Dark-eyed Junco was a regular backyard visitor: I marked it "present" on 29 days in January and on 24 days in February. Of its 174 "daily tallies," 93 of them came from our backyard.

[44] It is fascinating how bird populations can shift from year to year through migration. During my first winter of birding (the year recorded in this book), I saw literally hundreds of Pine Siskins. That is, I saw the Pine Siskin (as a species) on 121 occasions—but on many of those occasions I saw *lots* of Pine Siskins. On one occasion, walking through Whitley Place, I saw a din of 60–80 Pine Siskins in a single tree. And on multiple occasions I saw 20–30 of them. Yet, in my second year of birding, I

106	46. White-throated Sparrow
100	22. European Starling
96	56. Song Sparrow
95	16. Red-tailed Hawk
84	19. House Sparrow
82	100. Ruby-throated Hummingbird
80	36. Scissor-tailed Flycatcher
78	94. Green Heron
75	27. Ruby-crowned Kinglet
71	51. American Goldfinch
71	57. Red-winged Blackbird
71	82. Northern Rough-winged Swallow
67	58. Cedar Waxwing
65	33. Pied-billed Grebe
63	26. Northern Flicker
63	50. White-winged Dove
61	81. Brown-headed Cowbird
59	104. Chimney Swift
57	54. Northern Shoveler
55	42. Belted Kingfisher
55	49. Double-crested Cormorant
53	47. Brown Thrasher
50	93. Purple Martin
48	40. Great-tailed Grackle
47	24. Cooper's Hawk
46	39. Turkey Vulture
44	96. Snowy Egret
42	53. Ring-necked Duck
40	112. Common Nighthawk
37	20. Canada Goose
37	83. Cliff Swallow
36	3. Black Vulture
36	101. White-eyed Vireo

---

didn't see a single Pine Siskin in all of Collin County. Apparently, they went somewhere else for the winter that year.

36	113. Painted Bunting
35	25. Red-headed Woodpecker ("Woody")
35	38. Yellow-bellied Sapsucker
34	71. Orange-crowned Warbler ("Mabel")
34	107. Great Crested Flycatcher ("G.C.")
33	64. Lincoln's Sparrow
33	69. Gadwall
32	76. Lark Sparrow
31	52. Red-shouldered Hawk
31	75. White-breasted Nuthatch
30	98. Blue-gray Gnatcatcher
29	29. Killdeer
28	119. Yellow-crowned Night-Heron
27	95. Eastern Kingbird
27	115. Cattle Egret
26	35. American Coot
25	34. Rock Pigeon
23	65. Spotted Towhee[45]
22	60. Lesser Scaup
21	86. Hairy Woodpecker
20	48. American Wigeon
20	111. Western Kingbird
19	63. Harris's Sparrow
19	73. Hooded Merganser
19	168. Dickcissel
18	108. Yellow Warbler
17	121. Red-eyed Vireo
16	10. Common Grackle[46]

---

[45] Some common birds still rank very low on my list of daily tallies. This is because I went to locations in Oregon, Washington, and Utah only a few times—so most of the birds that I saw in those states rank very low in my tallies, even though they are common birds in those locations. The Spotted Towhee, for example, is very common in Oregon and Washington—but not common in Texas. So it is relatively low in my tallies.

[46] I must note: I saw some species much more frequently than these tallies indicate. Vultures, grackles, starlings, and pigeons—to name a few ex-

16	45. Brown Creeper
16	68. White-crowned Sparrow
16	123. Indigo Bunting
15	55. Fox Sparrow
15	74. Bewick's Wren
15	106. Nashville Warbler
15	110. Least Flycatcher
15	133. Black-capped Chickadee
14	72. Savannah Sparrow
13	87. Fish Crow
12	70. Bufflehead
11	61. Hermit Thrush
11	66. Golden-crowned Kinglet
11	88. Wood Duck
11	92. Black-chinned Hummingbird
11	118. Common Yellowthroat
10	89. Blue-winged Teal
10	130. Western Wood-Pewee
10	169. Least Sandpiper
9	37. Eastern Meadowlark
9	114. Spotted Sandpiper
9	160. Gray Catbird
8	41. Ring-billed Gull
8	67. Eurasian Collared-Dove
8	99. American Kestrel
8	102. Franklin's Gull

---

amples—are all very common, and I saw them very frequently. But I didn't record them every time I saw them. As mentioned, I was focused on creating tallies for my designated walks *at designated locations* (and for the birds that showed up in our backyard). So a bird like the Common Grackle, for example, received only 16 tallies for the entire year because —although I saw it nearly every day along the roadside or in a Walmart parking lot—I rarely saw it where I went walking, and I *never* saw it in our backyard. It seems odd to have a list showing that I saw the Common Grackle the same number of times that I saw the Indigo Bunting— because that simply isn't true. But so it goes.

8	109. Mississippi Kite
8	162. House Wren
7	59. Canvasback
7	77. Greater Yellowlegs
7	136. Black-headed Grosbeak
7	142. Violet-green Swallow
7	193. Baltimore Oriole
6	148. Marsh Wren
6	166. Yellow-billed Cuckoo
5	80. Chipping Sparrow
5	116. Willow Flycatcher
5	124. Little Blue Heron
5	127. Rufous Hummingbird[47]
5	137. California Quail
4	84. Osprey
4	135. Lesser Goldfinch
4	147. Tree Swallow
4	172. Loggerhead Shrike
4	174. Black-necked Stilt
3	14. Great Horned Owl
3	44. Blue-headed Vireo
3	62. Field Sparrow
3	91. Barred Owl
3	103. Greater Roadrunner
3	138. Wild Turkey
3	141. Chestnut-backed Chickadee
3	149. Brewer's Blackbird
3	152. Warbling Vireo
3	153. Black-billed Magpie
3	154. Common Raven
3	157. Pygmy Nuthatch
3	179. Caspian Tern

---

[47] The Rufous Hummingbird doesn't exist in Collin County, except maybe as it passes through during migration. But I still managed to see it on five separate occasions, on my trips to Oregon, Washington, and Utah.

3	182. White-faced Ibis
3	186. Woodhouse's Scrub-Jay
2	1. Pileated Woodpecker ("Frankie")
2	78. Green-winged Teal
2	79. Northern Pintail
2	117. Swainson's Thrush
2	128. Bald Eagle
2	131. Steller's Jay
2	132. California Scrub-Jay
2	140. Pacific-slope Flycatcher
2	143. Purple Finch
2	146. Cinnamon Teal
2	155. Mountain Chickadee
2	156. Red-breasted Nuthatch
2	158. Red Crossbill
2	159. Canyon Wren
2	161. Red-naped Sapsucker
2	167. Orchard Oriole
2	171. White Ibis
2	178. California Gull
2	180. American White Pelican
2	183. Bank Swallow
2	185. Yellow-headed Blackbird
2	189. Sandhill Crane
2	192. Olive-sided Flycatcher
2	194. Eastern Wood-Pewee
2	195. American Avocet
2	196. Lesser Yellowlegs
1	90. Yellow-throated Warbler[48]
1	97. Northern Harrier

---

[48] Of the last 32 birds that have just one tally—the birds that I saw or heard just once in my first year of birding—only three remain on my "Just Once" list, now that I'm completing my third year of birding. They are: (1) Wilson's Phalarope, (2) the Calliope Hummingbird and (3) the Broad-tailed Hummingbird.

1	105. Semipalmated Sandpiper
1	120. Blackburnian Warbler
1	122. Alder Flycatcher
1	125. Vaux's Swift
1	126. Anna's Hummingbird
1	129. Red-breasted Sapsucker
1	134. Bushtit
1	139. Sharp-shinned Hawk
1	144. Black-throated Gray Warbler
1	145. Wilson's Warbler
1	150. Western Gull
1	151. Brown Pelican
1	163. Western Bluebird
1	164. Veery
1	165. Bullock's Oriole
1	170. Long-billed Dowitcher
1	173. Swainson's Hawk
1	175. Western Grebe
1	176. Sora
1	177. Wilson's Phalarope
1	181. Black-crowned Night-Heron
1	184. Townsend's Solitaire
1	187. Calliope Hummingbird
1	188. Broad-tailed Hummingbird
1	190. Wilson's Snipe
1	191. Black Phoebe
1	197. Tricolored Heron
1	198. Anhinga
1	199. Clay-colored Sparrow
1	200. American Pipit

Index of Birds

Over 800 bird species can be found at least somewhat regularly in the United States, and this book devotes chapters to only 23 of them. I never discuss or even mention a wide variety of gulls, terns, sandpipers, seabirds, swallows, wrens, gamebirds, nuthatches, buntings, larks, or goatsuckers—to name only a few examples. But this index tracks every species that I *did* mention, as long as I mentioned it at least once by its proper name. (Note: this index does *not* include all the birds listed or mentioned in the Afterwords section.)

Bibliography

These are some of the books that I read (or at least perused) during my first year of birding—and that had an influence on this book either directly or indirectly.

A Conspiracy of Ravens, Samuel Fanous, Bodleian Library 2015.

All of Us: The Collected Poems, Raymond Carver, Knopf 1996.

An Exaltation of Larks, James Lipton, Penguin 1991.

At the Existentialist Café, Sarah Bakewell, Other Press 2016.

Bird Watcher's Bible, Ed. Jonathan Alderfer, National Geographic 2012.

Birds in Legend, Fable, and Folklore, Ernest Ingersoll, 1923.

Birds of Oregon: Field Guide, Stan Tekiela, Adventure 2001.

Birds of Texas: Field Guide, Stan Tekiela, Adventure 2004.

Boundaries, Henry Cloud & John Townsend, HarperCollins 2017.

Bright Wings: An Illustrated Anthology of Poems About Birds, Billy Collins (ed.), Columbia University Press 2013.

Codependent No More, Melody Beattie, Hazelden Publishing 1992.

Facing Codependence, Pia Mellody, HarperCollins 2003.

Feeling Great, David D. Burns, PESI 2020.

Good Birders Don't Wear White, Ed. Lisa White, Houghton Mifflin 2007.

H Is for Hawk, Helen Macdonald, Grove Press 2014.

How to Be an Adult in Relationships, David Richo, Shambhala 2002.

Leadership and Self-Deception, Arbinger Institute, Berrett-Koehler 2010.

Mrs. Moreau's Warbler: How Birds Got Their Names, Stephen Moss, Guardian Faber 2018.

Negotiating the Nonnegotiable, Daniel Shapiro, Penguin 2017.

Of a Feather: A Brief History of American Birding, Scott Weidensaul, Harcourt 2007.

On Wings of Song: Poems About Birds, Ed. J.D. McClatchy, Alfred A. Knopf 2000.

One Wild Bird at a Time, Bernd Heinrich, Houghton Mifflin 2016.

Selected Poems, Langston Hughes, Knopf 1993.

Set Boundaries, Find Peace, Nedra Glover Tawwab, Piatkus 2021.

Sisters of the Earth: Women's Prose & Poetry About Nature, Ed. Lorraine Anderson, Vintage Books 2003.

The Baseball 100, Joe Posnanski, Simon & Schuster 2021.

The Boy, the Mole, the Fox, and the Horse, Charlie Mackesy, HarperCollins 2019.

The Conscious Parent's Guide to Gender Identity, Darlene Tando, F+W Media 2016.

The Folklore of Birds, Laura C. Martin, Globe Pequot Press 1993.

The High-Conflict Couple, Alan E. Fruzzetti, New Harbinger 2006.

The Intimacy Factor, Pia Mellody, HarperCollins 2004.

The Nature Fix, Florence Williams, W.W. Norton 2017.

The New Rules of Marriage, Terrence Real, Ballantine Books 2008.

"The Origin and Meaning of Miles' Law," Rufus E. Miles, Jr., *Public Administration Review* 38:5 (1978).

The Poems of Gerard Manley Hopkins, Gerard Manley Hopkins, Oxford University Press 1970.

The Power of TED, David Emerald, Polaris 2016.

The Secret Language of Birds, Adele Nozedar, Harper 2006.

The Seven Principles for Making Marriage Work, John M. Gottman, Harmony 2015.

The Sibley Guide to Birds, David Allen Sibley, Knopf 2014.

The Turn to Ethics, Ed. Marjorie Garber, Beatrice Hanssen, and
    Rebecca L. Walkowitz, Routledge 2000.
They Tell of Birds: Chaucer, Spenser, Milton, Drayton, Thomas P.
    Harrison, Univ. of Texas Press 1956.
The Way It Is: New & Selected Poems, William Stafford, Graywolf
    Press 1999.
*This Is Water: Some Thoughts, Delivered on a Significant Occasion,
    about Living a Compassionate Life*, David Foster Wallace,
    Little Brown 2009.
Woodpeckers of North America, Frances Backhouse, Firefly 2005.
Zen Birding, David M. White & Susan M. Guyette, O-Books
    2010.

Acknowledgments

It took me longer than I thought it would, but I could not have finished this book without the love and support of my family—both my immediate family (Michele, Cameron, Mae, Jackson, Sophie, and Ruby) and my extended family (Mom & Dad, Jon & Jessica, Jake & Jessie, Joe & Shurisa, Jennie & Ian, Jane & Shawn, Jordan & Sunny, Jarrod & Cynthia, as well as Ray & Dana, Brian & Heidi, and Steve & Tango).

And of course my niece, Norah Steed, deserves a very special nod: her initial depiction of George (page 136) helped spark the idea for this project. And this book wouldn't be the same without her amazing artwork.

A special nod also goes to Mary Clearman Blew and Ron McFarland—and to some family members—for providing helpful feedback on earlier incarnations of this incantation.

Thank You, Reader

Finally, my sincerest and most bestest thanks to you, Dear Reader. Without you, this collection of pages is just a tree falling in the woods, soundless.

If you have a favorite chapter, or if any part of this book touched you in any way, I would love to hear about it. You can send emails to editor@ghowpress.com. You can also find book-related t-shirts, etc.—with Norah's great artwork!—using the QR code below. (A portion of the revenue from merchandise will go toward saving bird habitats.) And please consider writing a review online, wherever you buy your books.

Thank you, thank you, thank you.

– J.P.S.

About the Author

Jason Paul Steed holds a B.A. from Brigham Young University, an M.F.A. from the University of Idaho, a Ph.D. from the University of Nevada Las Vegas, and a J.D. from the University of Texas. He and his partner have five children. His stories, poems, and articles have appeared in a variety of publications. This is his first book.

Printed in the USA
CPSIA information can be obtained
at www.ICGtesting.com
LVHW021229090923
757249LV00022B/2

9 781960 554000